THE ART OF BASEBALL

SHELLY MEHLMAN DINHOFER

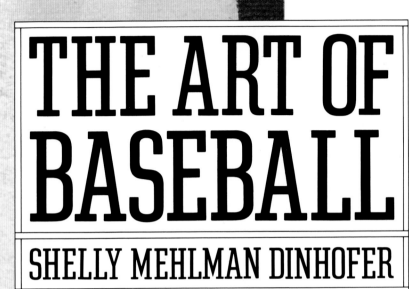

HARMONY BOOKS
NEW YORK

DEDICATION

This book is dedicated to Norman Dinhofer, who has shared my romance with baseball and my love of art for all the years of our continuing youth.

ACKNOWLEDGMENTS

I'd like to extend my gratitude to:

Peter Dinhofer, who formulated the outline without which this book could not have been written and who taught me that a beloved old typewriter doesn't measure up to a well-programmed computer.

Bill Gladstone for his warm encouragement, technical expertise, and total joy in the game.

Michael Boodro for always knowing when three adjectives were two too many.

Michael Pietsch, my editor, for his professionalism and unflagging support.

My family, friends, and associates who gave of their love and their trust in a time of travail.

My special thanks to the museums, artists, and collectors who were so interested in the linked theme of art and baseball and so gracious in allowing their works of art to be reproduced.

Designer: Seymour Chwast, The Pushpin Group

Associate Designer: Roxanne Slimak

Copyright © 1990 by Shelly Mehlman Dinhofer

Published by Harmony Books, a division of Crown Publishers, Inc.
201 East 50th Street, New York, New York 10022

Harmony and colophon are trademarks of Crown Publishers, Inc.

Manufactured in Japan

Library of Congress Cataloging-in-Publication Data

Dinhofer, Shelly.
The art of baseball: the great American game in painting, sculpture and folk art / by Shelly Dinhofer.
p. cm.
1. Baseball in art. 2. Art, American. 3. Art, Modern — 20th century — United States. I. Title.
N8217.B36D56 1989
704.9′49796357′0973 — dc20   89-11229
CIP

ISBN 0-517-57567-1
10 9 8 7 6 5 4 3 2 1   MAR 1 7 2008

First Edition

CONTENTS

INTRODUCTION
THE GRAND GAME
OF BASEBALL

THE NINETEENTH CENTURY:
TRADITIONAL IMAGERY
AND THE
AMERICAN EXPERIENCE

1900–1930:
THE ROLLER COASTER
DECADES

1930–1950:
GOVERNMENT AND
THE GAME

1950–1988:
BUSINESS
PLAYS BALL

BASEBALL ENTERS
THE CULTURAL
MAINSTREAM

EPILOGUE

LIST OF ILLUSTRATIONS

ARTISTS' INDEX

THE GRAND GAME OF BASEBALL

Baseball, the Great American National Pastime, is a straightforward, lively game strenuously played, according to long-established rules, in the warmth of the summer sun. It is a sandlot game in quiet town squares and backwaters, a game of stickball on the hard pavements of busy urban streets, a spectator sport in vast impersonal arenas. The game requires both individual ingenuity and team interaction and has come to symbolize initiative, competition, and the enterprising, combative spirit of commercial success.

Ritual ball games were recognized as crowd pleasers even in ancient cultures. Often they represented reenactments of the life cycle with its traditional rewards and harsh punishments. The fiercely aggressive, bitterly fought seasonal games featured gladiatorial bravura, teams fighting to the death, and unpredictable results, much to the gratification of the onlookers.

In pre-Columbian Mexico, huge ballparks, built to accommodate the eager throngs, were incorporated into temple sites. The games were regarded as ceremonial events, with profound religious connotations, performed at the command of a panoply of gods. In some cultures, the losers were decapitated, their heads mounted around the ballpark, symbolic of victory and absolute control.

The Romans played entirely different games. Central Sicily's Piazza Armerina [Fig. 1] houses the ruins of a grand hunting lodge. The mosaics in one special room are representations of a group of seductive

bikini-clad young women playing catch ball for the entertainment of the attendant nobles.

In a less patrician environment, the Plains Indians of North America regarded their ball games as nothing less than war. The wild melees and violent confrontations that ensued give evidence that speed, strength, ferocity and determination, rather than skill, were the essential components for victory. George Catlin (1796–1872), who documented the Indians' customs in prose and paintings, depicted the typically chaotic, frenzied atmosphere in his painting "Ball Play of the Choctaw-Ball Up" (1834–35) [Fig. 6].

Ball games, derived from the pagan past, became part of Christian rites and were played with pomp and ceremony in French and English church courtyards.

Figures, bat and ball in hand, were even used as decorative adjuncts in medieval manuscripts [Fig. 4]. Gradually, the games assumed a recreational aspect.

In the mid-eighteenth century, rounders, a popular English schoolboy game, was illustrated in a children's book of verse, *A Pretty Little Pocket Book* (1820) [Fig. 3]. This game crossed the Atlantic and took hold among the colonial elite. Rounders is actually a game of tag with a ball thrown at the running target. It is still played in England, but today mostly by schoolgirls.

In her novel *Northanger Abbey*, published in 1818, Jane Austen described with mild disapproval an active young lad who preferred cricket and "base-ball" to anything else. And in 1829, Oliver Wendell Holmes played a game with bat, ball, and bases on a diamond-shaped area in Har-

1. *Roman Mosaic, Piazza Armerina, Sicily*, fourth century

2. Illustration from the Egyptian Tomb of Beni Hassan

PLAYING BALL

3. Illustration from *A Pretty Little Pocket Book*, 1820

vard Yard. Shortly thereafter, members of exclusive men's clubs in several eastern cities were eagerly participating in this leisure activity.

What rules there were differed from region to region until the fall of 1845, when a bank teller, Alexander J. Cartwright, under the auspices of a group of New York gentlemen, formally organized the Knickerbocker Base Ball Club and codified the rules of the game. Included in the twenty rules were the following familiar ones: three outs in an inning; bases equidistant and standardized; and, for the sake of gentlemanly decorum, an impartial mediator, the umpire. In the interest of minimizing injuries, the base runners were to be tagged for the out by an opposing player with the ball in hand, rather than have the ball thrown directly at them. Uniforms were declared essential as indicators of team spirit, cooperation, and neatness. As the ball was thrown underhand and barehanded, gloves would then have been considered a sign of cowardice.

On a bright, windless June afternoon in 1846, at the Elysian Fields in Hoboken, New Jersey, the Knickerbockers played against the New York Base Ball Club in the first officially documented match. The players were newly uniformed and poised for action. Gentlemen in top hats and boaters watched from the sidelines. Families in their formal finery crowded together at the field's perimeters, and fancy carriages lined the roadway as far as the eye could see. Twenty years later, in 1866, that carefree image, securely locked in time, was widely disseminated by the publishing firm of Currier and Ives in a full-color lithograph, "The American National Game of Baseball [Fig. 7]." Although the Knickerbockers lost ignominiously, on that momentous day the game of baseball left the rarified atmosphere of the rich and entered the popular culture.

Baseball has enabled each succeeding generation to discover and establish its own cultural identity within the framework of the American experience. The literature of baseball is vast and timeless and well read; consider the stark dramatic novels of Bernard Malamud and Mark Harris, Ring Lardner's tales of the Twenties and Roger Angell's stories of the Eighties, Franklin P. Adams's charming ditties and the serious poetry of Marianne Moore. Dramatists, playwrights, humorists, and lyricists— almost everyone who writes has written at some time about baseball. The English language has been expanded through baseball's special vernacular. Sportswriters provide the descriptive analyses; photographers, the visual documentation. Songs are written with fluid grace and staccato beat. "Take Me Out to the Ball Game" still vies with the "Star Spangled Banner" for first place. It is all a cultural feast for the baseball public.

The art of baseball, however, occupies a separate place, transcending the game itself. It brings forward in timeless imprint the artist's interpretation of the color and form, the physical interaction, the sheer energy of the game. Its history reflects the players' grand theater, the fans' emotional

4. Illustration from a Medieval Manuscript

5. Illustration from *The Book of Sports*, 1834

6. George Catlin, *Ball Play of the Choctaw-Ball Up*, 1834–35

attachment, and the owners' business acumen.

As the ease and spontaneity of outdoor play gave way to structure and definition, and baseball as we have come to know it evolved, artists turned from scenes of light-hearted figures and pastoral charm to the harsh, complex reality of urban street life. Baseball's basic design changed gradually, adapting to economic and population growth, to vast steel and concrete arenas, to the perennial springtime of the West and Southwest. From the sixty fiercely competitive teams of the National Association of Base Ball Players to the formally constituted National League, from a series of small poorly designed federations to the steadfast American League, from segregated teams for segregated audiences to total integration, the game's evolution has been mirrored in the stylistic diversity of the visual arts.

This book is a personal tribute from an art historian and ardent unregenerate Brooklyn Dodgers baseball fan. It stems from a childhood in the bleachers of Ebbets Field, clutching soggy, delicious hot dogs, shrieking in joy or dismay as the distant figures leapt, soared, swooped with heart-stopping mobility and grace. From the boxes to the far-reaching stands, there was unanimity of choice and loyalty beyond expectation. It was always the home team, our team, the Brooklyn Dodgers. I learned basic mathematics and logic from those early games, memorizing the statistics, computing the odds, evaluating the opposition. I learned how to look at action from afar, to watch reality become abstraction in the hot glaze of the summer sun, to actually see how the fusing of light and color could alter my perception.

The art of baseball was a revelation. I discovered that virtually every major American artist had a baseball-related image tucked within a body of work, whether it was a simple descriptive drawing or a grand metaphorical statement. In 1987, I curated an exhibition for the Museum of the Borough of Brooklyn, Brooklyn, New York, an institution I had founded and directed. Aptly titled "The Grand Game of Baseball...and the Brooklyn Dodgers" the exhibition struck an immediate, amazingly responsive chord. Fans who had never before seriously viewed a work of art flocked to study the baseball images, while those primarily interested in this informal survey of nineteenth- and twentieth-century American art were caught by the electric atmosphere of the game itself. The conversations were sometimes hilarious, more often mutually informative. Like most baseball ventures, it was a gratifying success.

Organized baseball has flourished as the country's major spectator sport. Indeed, the lusty cry "Play ball" is second only to the national anthem in patriotic fervor. And it has continued so, despite all the vicissitudes of major conflicts, illegitimate schemes, and historic scandals, despite big-business machinations and bad decisions. Under the artificial lights of night-time play and airless domed stadiums, baseball continues because it remains the best and most exciting playground of the American imagination.

7. Currier and Ives, *The American National Game of Base Ball*, 1866

ATIONAL GAME OF BASE BALL.

CHAMPIONSHIP AT THE ELYSIAN FIELDS, HOBOKEN, N.J.

8. John George Brown, *Put It There*, n.d.

The Nineteenth Century:

Traditional Imagery and the American Experience

Part One

9. Unidentified Artist, *Boy With Ball and Bat*, 1844

10. David Gilmour Blythe, *Youth*, 1865

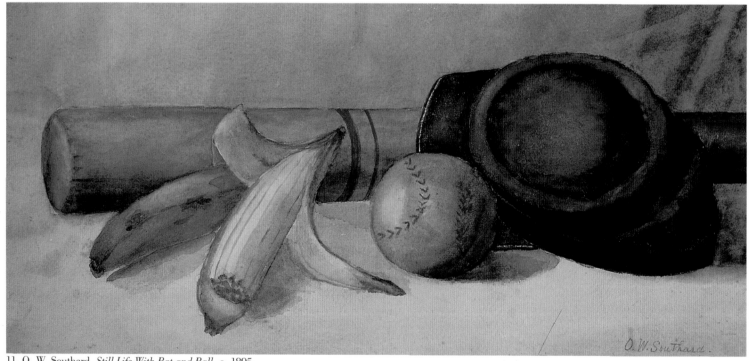

11. O. W. Southard, *Still Life With Bat and Ball*, c. 1895

Baseball captured the attention of artists long before it became the national pastime. With its outdoor setting, numerous figures, varied palette, and spontaneous action, the game was recognized as a phenomenon rich in aesthetic possibilities. It was also the means of integrating American popular culture within the traditional European fine-arts subject matter of landscape, portraiture, and genre scenes.

From its inception, the game supplied the nineteenth-century American artist with provocative themes and icons that reflected a unique American experience. Its imagery was imbued with a youthful optimism, an idealism metaphoric of the new republic. Though identified with and trained in European sensibilities, such as the confining grandeur of Paris's beaux-arts academies, or the somber dark hues of Munich's art schools, America's painters and sculptors turned their stylistic concerns to this fledgling sport and its distinctly homegrown vernacular. They were intrigued by its dramatic action and colorful atmosphere, its humor and frustration, and especially by the hordes of spectators eating with gusto, drinking with abandon, quarrelsome but content to be out in the sun expressing themselves, at one with their team. The game's vitality was played out across countless canvases, challenging painters to capture its energy and spirit, commanding the versatility of sculptors, enhancing America's static figurative tradi-

12. Currier and Ives, *The National Game*, 1860

PORTRAITURE AND STILL LIFE

tion. The artists, however, were not simply viewers, removed from the tumult. Some were participants, others proved to be among baseball's foremost fans and most acute observers. They portrayed the graceful, easy movements of the players. They depicted the emotional variables, the euphoric excitement of the winners, the dejection of the losers, the grandstanding and posturing, the transient anger. These artists placed the game within the nation's visual and cultural history.

Portraiture remained the staple for professional and itinerant artists alike. It provided the financial support for stylistic experimentation and development of new ideas. The youthful aspect of the game is evident in the formal portrait by an unknown painter, "Boy With Ball and Bat" (1844) [Fig. 9]. The subject, solemn and attentive, carefully clothed and combed, holds tight the equipment necessary for a

game of rounders, perhaps. Undoubtedly a commission, the painting is a simple, straightforward presentation, sensitive in expression and mood, a competent, disciplined portrayal with an English perspective. It is reflective of the concern for childhood and its accoutrements which prevailed at that time; but the unmistakable ball and bat, the determined yet pensive look add another dimension.

By the middle of the nineteenth century, with artists reaping the financial benefits of

UNION PRISONERS AT SAL

DRAWN FROM NATURE BY ACT. MAJOR OTTO BOETT

Lith of SARONY MAJOR & KNAPP 449 Broadway N.York.

13. Otto Boetticher, *Union Prisoners at Salisbury, N.C.*, 1863

the public's taste for simple, clear, direct representations of family and home, still-life paintings were second only to portraits as best-sellers. The use of everyday objects lent an intimate, decorative touch to what were often pedestrian replicas of the Dutch and French "natur morte" (fruit and crockery) paintings of the previous century. An unusually idealistic evocation of youth's passage is David Gilmour Blythe's (1815–1865) still life "Youth" (1865) [Fig. 10], whose symbolism is obvious, if not overwhelming. Among the appurtenances of boyhood are a primer, a partially eaten slice of bread, a pocketknife, marbles, a firecracker, peppermint candy, an hourglass, almost full, and a baseball, centrally focused, distinctly larger than the other objects, reflecting the physical ability and energy of youth. Daylight streams from the upper right-hand corner toward a gathering of budding roses, and in the background the United States Capitol dome emerges from the mist as a continuing symbol of hope. Blythe, whose last desperate years were spent in Pittsburgh's growing industrial sprawl, was long considered the painter of pessimism. His usual repertoire of oddly formed, ragged, evil-looking street urchins epitomized life's darker side. Here, however, the joyful paraphernalia of youth and its innocence is joined with a patriotic vision of the future indicating the promise of ambition (for this painter, at least), an interesting anomaly. "Youth" and a companion piece depicting old age were commissioned by a Pittsburgh merchant and collector, Christian H. Wolffe, for a mere twenty-five dollars, frames included.

POLITICS AND PATRIOTISM

Baseball's imagery was easily extended to the rather untidy political scene of the 1860s. As a metaphor for individual worth and integrity, or as a means of pointing to personal foibles with deadly humor, it could be quickly read and understood, even by an unsophisticated electorate. Currier and Ives, responsive as always to events of immediate interest, produced a print entitled with obvious intent, "The National Game. Three 'Outs' and One 'Run'. Abraham Winning the Ball" (1860) [Fig. 12], for mass distribution. It depicted the four Presidential candidates, Abraham Lincoln, John Bell, Stephen Douglas, and John C. Breckenridge, as baseball players dispensing with the usual election year rhetoric and just getting down to basics. As media hype, it was the thirty-second tele-

14. Thomas Eakins, *Baseball Players Practicing*, 1875

vision spot of its day and very effective.

While the Civil War dampened the spirit and enterprise of baseball enthusiasts and halted its rapidly expanding professional base, the game continued to be absorbed into the prevailing popular culture. On December 25, 1862, the largest crowd ever gathered to see a sporting event in the United States, more than forty thousand Union soldiers, lustily cheered a game between teams from the 165th New York Volunteer Infantry and Duryea's Zouaves.

The public's demand for war information was so great that newsweeklies and magazines proliferated, wildly vying for the services of artists to ensure adequate coverage of the carnage. The art of illustration developed dramatically during the early 1860s. Illustrators were permitted to visit the fragmented war fronts and to recreate virtually everything that suited the reporter's story or the artist's fancy. They depicted the war's relentless horror for insatiable readers and, although the more ghoulish presentations of death and destruction dominated the news, the artists did try on occasion to provide a "leitmotif" to offset the war's despair.

This is the apparent basis for Otto Boetticher's (b. about 1816–died after 1864) lithograph "Union Prisoners at Salisbury, N.C." (1863) [Fig. 13]. It could be any peaceful village on a Sunday: the centered diamond, the lively figure running the bases, groups of spectators, some watching intently, others just lounging about. The barracks are in a semicircle, neatly drawn and positioned amid foliage, with only a picket fence separating the players from the village just beyond. It's a very civilized scene, indeed, and an excellent propaganda ploy for the Confederacy. Actually, Boetticher made the drawing while incarcerated in the Confederate prison in 1862. It was later adapted as a lithograph and distributed by the printing firm of Sarony, Major, and Knapp.

THE AMERICAN VERNACULAR

With the war over and the Industrial Revolution continuing to enrich the rapidly expanding middle class, the game of baseball regained its momentum as the premier American sport. Artists who could afford to do so were absorbing European culture, trading off the excitement of open-air competitions for the stifling environment of rigid studio discipline. Some of the artists,

15. William Morris Hunt, *The Ball Players*, 1877

dominated by a European viewpoint, remained abroad as expatriates; others, though exhilarated by their introduction to old masters and new techniques, returned to the American scene.

Thomas Eakins (1844–1916) is perhaps the most representative of those artists who adapted the rigors of academic painting to his own distinct and individual style. Eakins studied for three years with the highly acclaimed French academic painter Jean-Léon Gérôme at the Ecole des Beaux-Arts in Paris. Gérôme dedicated himself to the rich themes of Near Eastern splendor and historic events. His work displayed mastery of form and factual precision. Eakins, Gérôme's favorite student, returned to Philadelphia and to his consuming family life with a deepening interest in figure studies: figures in movement, in contemplation, in the expressive activity of sporting events, boxing, sculling, swimming, diving, and, in a single instance, the game of baseball. His watercolor "Baseball Players Practicing" (1875) [Fig. 14], which he exhibited with pride that same year at a watercolor show in New York, is primarily concerned with the immediacy of a tense moment in the game. The stances of the players are rigid with anticipation, an urgency and suspense left forever unresolved. The work is deceptively simple. There is an airiness, an infusion of light which removes it from the academic formula. The artist describes the content in a letter to his good friend and traveling companion, the Philadelphia painter and teacher Earl Shinn: "…The moment is just after the batter has taken his bat, before the ball leaves the pitcher's hand. They are portraits of Athletic boys, a Philadelphia club. I conceive that they are pretty well drawn. Ball players are very fine in their build. They are the same stuff as bull fighters only bull fighters are older and a trifle stronger perhaps. I think I will try to make a base ball picture some day in oil. It will admit of fine figure painting…" If Eakins ever did complete an oil painting with baseball as a theme, it has not come to public attention. True to his insistence on

accuracy, Eakins carefully identified the Philadelphia Athletics as the club engaged in baseball practice. He neglected to note, however, that the players portrayed were Wes Fisler, first baseman, and John Clapp, catcher.

FIGURES IN THE LANDSCAPE: BARBIZON TECHNIQUES AND HIGH ART

The broad strokes of William Morris Hunt's (1824–1879) "The Ball Players" (1877) [Fig. 15] convey an entirely different message. Hunt, an articulate, enthusiastic exponent of "high art," had lived and worked with Jean-François Millet and the French Barbizon painters isolated in the forest of Fontainebleau. Although he left France for his native Boston in 1855, Hunt continued to teach and to work in the painterly manner he appreciated. Thus his painting of three men in an open field playing stickball remains clearly expressive of the Barbizon techniques he had absorbed some twenty years before, capturing the elusive mood and spirit of the game while leaving the details deliberately muted and indistinct. The figures, incongruously clothed in dark suits and straw hats, are playing the game with a lackadaisical detachment. There is an elegaic quality to the quiet landscape into which they have been incorporated.

Even if the subject chosen was as unmistakably American as baseball, the imposition of "high art"'s exacting standards on taste is evident in the post-war period. Perhaps it was the influence of those dealer-artists living abroad; more likely, however, it was the art patrons themselves who were becoming more sophisticated, more traveled, more aware of diverse European movements.

While American artists were developing richer aesthetic values, they continued to experiment with the stylish imagery inherent in the game of baseball. John La Farge (1835–1910), a student of Hunt's, also espoused "high art," developing therein his own well-defined neoclassical vocabulary. His cosmopolitan interests were further

16. John La Farge, *Standing Dance Representing the Game of Ball*, 1890–91

17. Douglas Tilden, *The Baseball Player*, 1888–89

advanced by extensive travel to more exotic climes, notably the Orient and the South Seas. La Farge, an intelligent, facile painter, was able to resolve for himself conflicts engendered by his concept of the mythic grandeur of the ideal and the solid respectability of the representational elements pursued by so many of his colleagues. He simply combined the two in irreverent fantasies. La Farge's watercolor "Standing Dance Representing the Game of Ball" (1890–91) [Fig. 16] depicts classical figures, women in diaphanous skirts and partially clad men, moving through a romantic green glade in an idyllic South Seas locale, but, nevertheless, playing baseball. His sensitive use of color as well as the strength of his drawing gives a certain credibility to this imagined scene.

HEROIC IMAGES: CLASSICAL CANONS TO GENRE

Perhaps the strongest, most evocative work of art of this neoclassical genre, an assertive declaration of the stature of the individual image, is Douglas Tilden's (1860–1935) bronze sculpture "The Baseball Player" (1888–89) [Fig. 17]. An avid sports fan and college athlete, Tilden clearly understood the importance of the game of baseball to the American psyche. Although scarlet fever rendered him deaf and mute at age five, he became a student of painting, drawing, and sculpture in his native California, moved on to New York and the National Academy of Design, and then, in 1888, to Paris, where he absorbed the nuances of France's decorative sculptural tradition in the studios of Paul Chopin and Emanuel Fremient. He never lost sight of his origins, however, and the strength of his American experience is particularly apparent in this remarkable sports image.

The figure stands clear-eyed and intent, his shirt moving with unexpected grace as he prepares to throw the ball in the designated underhand motion. His stance—left arm bent across the chest, upper torso thrust forward—projects the illusion of an immediate action. Though based on classical canons of balance and weight, the figure epitomizes the idealized hero so relevant to his times. In keeping with Tilden's sense of reality, the face is a carefully modeled self-portrait. The original life-size work was cast in plaster. Replicated in bronze, it was accepted for exhibition in the Paris Salon of 1890 and, subsequently, was the only American work shown at San Francisco's Art Loan Exhibition of European masters the following year. Purchased from the

exhibition by an admirer, W. E. Brown of the Southern Pacific Railroad Company, the sculpture was immediately donated to the city of San Francisco. This monumental work remains on permanent display in Golden Gate National Park. The plaster version was later exhibited at Chicago's World Columbian Exposition.

As an amalgam of American taste and French technical expertise, the work excited considerable interest, so much so, in fact, that art collectors and connoisseurs clamored for reduced replicas from the Paris foundry of E. Gruet. Only two have come to view, however, one currently in the collection of the National Baseball Hall of Fame and Museum at Cooperstown, New York, the other in private hands. In response to the continuing demand, Tiffany's of New York ordered slightly smaller versions from the same foundry.

Sculptors, concerned with capturing the ease and freedom of an individual action, projected the players in fanciful dance-like positions. Jonathan Scott Hartley (1845–1912), for example, presented his "The Baseball Player" (1886) [Fig. 18] in a lithe, leaping movement, a weightless figure effortlessly retrieving a ball in space, a distinct contrast to Tilden's solidly grounded symbol of strength and determination.

The neoclassical tradition was further enhanced by artists who visited the great European museum collections and found there the technical virtuosity and aesthetic of antiquity. A student at the Pennsylvania Academy of the Fine Arts, Isaac Broome (1835–1922) was on the traditional grand European tour when he discovered for himself the classic beauty of Greek and Etruscan vases. Trained as a sculptor, Broome worked closely with Thomas Crawford on the execution of the statues for the pediment of the United States Capitol. However, his interest in the technical aspects of the potter's art and its creative implications remained the motivating factor in his art life.

As soon as the Civil War ended and economic opportunities became more viable, Broome opened a ceramics manufactory in Pittsburgh. While there, he developed a close friendship with the painter David Gilmour Blythe. A watercolor painted by Blythe in 1865 depicts the two friends standing in front of J. J. Gillespie's frame shop, Blythe's gallery at the time. Broome is portrayed as a debonair, prosperous gentleman with full beard, top hat, and cane, very much in charge. He produced architectural ornaments, fountains, and vases for an affluent clientele before returning to sculpture and portrait paint-

18. Jonathan Scott Hartley, *The Baseball Player*, 1886

31

ing. In 1871, he opened another terra-cotta factory in Brooklyn, New York, developing a reputation for innovative ceramic design.

In 1876, numerous celebrations of the nation's 100th birthday rang with pride and achievement. The grandest of these, The United States International Exhibition, known thereafter as The Centennial, was to be held in Philadelphia. Broome was approached by the Ott and Brewer Company, prominent ceramicists of Trenton, New Jersey, shortly before The Centennial was organized, and was engaged to prepare unique designs especially for exhibition. The comprehensive international exposition drew vast crowds; approximately ten million people visited halls filled with machinery, machine-made products, and horticultural exhibits. There was a special Women's Pavilion, and a section for The Arts and Industries. Rather than a simple affirmation of historic values, The Centennial was dedicated to the vitality of the present and the proud expectations for the future.

Broome designed the "Baseball Vase" (1876) [Fig. 21], actually a covered urn, as a representative symbol of the national pastime and in homage to the spirit of optimism and fair play that America represented. In true neoclassical fashion, he emphasized the relationship of democracy to the classical civilizations of antiquity. He positioned freestanding players—a pitcher, batter, and catcher—against background scenes of the game in low relief. A laurel wreath encircling the neck of the urn gives evidence of baseball's relationship, in spirit at least, to the games of ancient Rome. The American eagle atop the lid exemplifies the patriotic spirit. Broome was honored with several medals for the originality of his designs and for his successful technical experiments. The urn was made of unglazed bisque called American parian ware because of its resemblance to the creamy white shading and texture of marble. In honor of his expertise, Broome was appointed United States Commissioner of Ceramics for the 1878 Universal Exposition in Paris.

While style remained an issue and figurative studies provided an ongoing attraction, artists used baseball's eclectic viewpoint to explore other areas, to expand public interest, and to profit by it.

Genre painting, depictions of people engaged in ordinary everyday activity, was a popular antidote to the more demanding intellectual appeal of "high art." Sentiment and a high moral tone permeated much of the content, but the affluent middle class, hungry for wall decorations, for art forms to

19. Isaac Broome, *Pitcher*, 1876

20. William Merritt Chase, *The Baseball Player*, c. 1872

21. Isaac Broome, *Baseball Vase*, 1876

22. W. P. Snyder, *Collegiate Game of Baseball*, 1889

which they could easily relate, responded eagerly. The diversity of city life supplied an immediate visual gratification, a heightened excitement not evident in the calm serenity of contemporary landscapes. Although many of the paintings were derivative of Dutch and Flemish eighteenth-century imagery, the American urban experience elicited the strongest, most positive reaction. The true qualities of the time, social displacement and economic inequity, were, of course, not considered felicitous subjects for household decoration. The "all is well" syndrome was the key to an artist's success, and baseball was a sure and viable vehicle.

The work of the influential genre painter John George Brown (1831–1913) is clearly reflective of this point of view. Brown's sentimental portrayal "Put It There" (n.d.) [Fig. 8] shows a young street urchin grinning malevolently as he demonstrates the action of the moment. His frontal stance and direct unflinching gaze, his one bare fist pounding the mitt, project a provocative invitation to the viewer to play ball ...or else. Brown's paintings of young boys participating in outdoor activities were in

such great demand, and he was so prolific, that they soon became rote images, devoid of any personal statement. Inexpensive chromolithographs of his work were produced in large quantities, obviously successful in their appeal to a mass audience.

Baseball's lighthearted imagery, its costumes and poses, were momentarily enticing even to artists whose serious intent lay elsewhere. William Merritt Chase's (1849–1916) simple student drawing "The Baseball Player" (c. 1872) [Fig. 20], a slight and charming quick study, suggests a pleasant memory in the midst of stricter endeavors. Chase, who had been studying at the National Academy of Design, left for the more formal atmosphere and training of the Munich Academy. He returned, a master teacher, eagerly sought after by generations of students. Later he developed his own light and airy impressionist palette for which he is best known.

Even in the latter part of the nineteenth century, when entrance to the stands required only the price of admission and behavior be damned, artists continued to portray baseball fans as retaining a sense of decorum, clearly unrepresentative of the

actual facts. Nevertheless, in popular illustration, there remained the men, neat and tidy in attire, and the ladies in their well-groomed best, beautifully coiffured with large broad-brimmed hats, blocking all views, but very much seen. *Harper's Weekly*, the widely distributed newsmagazine, conveyed the playful atmosphere of handsomely gowned women, and some equally fashionable men, in relaxed poses at a "Collegiate Game of Baseball" (1889) [Fig. 22], as drawn by W. P. Snyder (n.d.). The number of women present could also have signified a "Ladies' Day" at the ballpark, since this, the oldest promotion in baseball, was already an established practice in 1889. In a similar vein, artist-illustrator Jay Hambidge's (1867–1924) delicately toned four-color print "Crowd at the Polo Grounds" (1895) [Fig. 23] catches the spirited crowd in all its finery, top hats and bowlers, straw skimmers and mutton-sleeved blouses. The New York Giants are playing to a capacity crowd on their home ground. It is a boisterous gathering. With mouths agape and arms flailing, the fans are giving clear evidence of their displeasure with the action on the field.

23. Jay Hambidge, *Crowd at the Polo Grounds*, 1895

24. Nickolas Muray, *Babe Ruth (George Herman Ruth)*, c.1927

1900-1930:

The Roller Coaster
Decades

*Part
Two*

25. Robert Henri, *George Luks Playing Baseball*, 1904

By the beginning of the twentieth century, the impact of European academic painting had diminished. Rural lifestyles, serene vistas, charming sentiment, and the leisure activities of polite society were giving way to the harsh reality of the industrial landscape. The action, the subject matter, the very nature of city life were enacted on the bustling streets. A purely American dynamic came into focus and American Realism was the artists' reaction.

THE ASHCAN SCHOOL

In Philadelphia, a group of four hard-working, hard-playing newspaper illustrators, William Glackens, George Luks, Everett Shinn, and John Sloan, all of whom worked for the *Philadelphia Press*, came under the influence of an articulate, debonair painter, Robert Henri (1865–1929). Henri had lived in Paris for some time, studying at the Academie Julian and the Ecole des Beaux-Arts. While there, he was introduced to the diffused light, interactive color tones, and plein air palette of Impressionism. He rejected the movement. He was drawn instead to the dark tonality and sudden highlights of the Dutch master Frans Hals, whose works he discovered in Haarlem and elsewhere in Holland. Considered an extraordinary teacher as well as a painter, Henri created an art circle composed of his illustrator friends and other devotees, first in Philadelphia and then in New York. He encouraged them to paint the rowdy turbulence, the working-class optimism of the American city scene. Eventually, they became known as the Ashcan School in honor of the many ash bins lining the city streets.

Of the four, the man who adhered to Henri's manner of painting most assiduously was the irrepressible, hard-drinking son of an artistic Pennsylvania Dutch family, George Luks (1866–1933). Luks could as easily be found in a saloon as behind an easel...or on the ball field. He was renowned for his caustic tongue, great binges, and devotion to those inhabiting the dark side of the city.

On August 12, 1904, the staid Henri drew an affectionate cartoon of Luks, "George Luks Playing Baseball," [Fig. 25] as a paunchy little figure with hair unkempt and nose mottled, grinning venomously and preparing to toss a baseball. Henri bowed to Luks's dexterity on the mound in a droll postscript: "Dear Luks," he noted on the drawing, "...I hear you are a great

26. George Luks, *Boy with Baseball*, c. 1925

27. George Luks, *Base-Ball at Nunkie-Now!! Ah! Ah!!* (Dr. Andrew Green Ford Playing Baseball), c. 1916

28. Charles Dana Gibson, *Everybody Up—Seventh Inning Stretch*, 1913

pitcher. They say few balls were hit until late in the afternoon."

That Luks was also attracted to Hals's dark-toned palette is apparent in his "Boy With Baseball" (c. 1925) [Fig. 26]. The youngster, fresh faced and bright eyed, with startling red cheeks, is posed informally, hands thrust deep in his pockets. His clean white shirt and short pants are offset by the baseball hat set askew on his head and the baseball casually placed on the settee beside him. He gazes out expectantly, eager to dart away from the somber backdrop and get on with the game. Luks, who had drawn comic strips for the *New York World*, had his own brand of illustrational humor; it was as outrageous as it was simplistic. His cartoon with the curious title "Base-Ball at Nunkie-Now!! Ah! Ah!!" (Dr. Andrew Green Ford Playing Base-Ball) (c. 1916) [Fig. 27] depicts a joyously uninhibited figure, dressed in baseball clothing and grinning demoniacally, leaping through the air, having just hit a home run, no doubt. Below him, moving frantically and apparently jumping for joy, are stick figures of his teammates and friends. It is obviously a very quick study, drawn on site, but it reflects the wild energy of the man and his rather hysterical reaction to the game.

To say that George Bellows (1882–1925), the foremost second-generation realist, had a ravenous appetite for baseball is no overstatement. By the age of ten, Bellows was playing stickball on the streets of his native Columbus, Ohio. He joined his high-school baseball team and continued team play at Ohio State University. He played semi-pro ball, as shortstop, during summer vacations for pleasure and profit and was so good at the game that the Cincinnati Reds offered him a contract. After serious consideration, he refused, because, while baseball and art were equal passions, he was eager to enter the sophisticated art scene of New York. Bellows studied with Robert Henri from 1904 to 1906 and adapted to his realist concepts with ease and instant success. He found his images in the kids diving into tepid waters on a sweltering afternoon, in the boxers striving for achievement, in the people crowding tenements and streets. His broad brush strokes and vivid colors gave his canvases a quality of immediacy. In spite of his inclination to join every baseball game he happened upon, Bellows never exhibited a major painting of the game.

29. Frank Hoffman, *Safe at Home*, 1925

FANS AND OTHER FOLLOWERS

Running counter to continuing depictions of civility in the stands, Bellows's crayon drawing "Take Him Out" (1906) [Fig. 33] is a caricature study of vitriol and anger, however nonthreatening. According to his view, though genteel spectators might still occupy boxes, the stands were filled by the raucous, intemperate fans eager to vent their emotions. In this composition, facial contortions and figurative tension empha-size the frenzied atmosphere. Whoever the pitcher was, he must have floated one ball too many past cloud nine to have inspired "Take Him Out."

In contrast, civility was the very password of Charles Dana Gibson's (1855–1919) "girls," whose decorative images filled the pages of contemporary magazines and calendars. The woman he portrays in "Everybody Up—Seventh Inning Stretch" (1913) [Fig. 28] is indistinguishable from many others he has illustrated—stretching languorously, showing off her wasp waist and stylish dress. The bodily contortions of her two male companions are presented with humorous intent. They could just as well have risen from a box at the opera as a box at a baseball game. Gibson's popularity was such, however, that the subjects were readily accepted and admired. The seventh-inning stretch remains an integral part of the game. It began somewhere back in the annals of baseball lore and was intended to allow the spectators a bit of exercise and a release of tension, performed in the most dignified manner possible.

As the emphasis on classically correct images became less pronounced, artists began to portray the growing ethnic diversity of the urban population with sympathy as well as caricature. Maurice Sievan's (1898–1981) drawing "Newsboy" (1914) [Fig. 31] depicts a boy, papers aloft, gleefully running down a crowded tenement-lined street on New York's Lower East Side, shouting out the headlines, proclaiming the "Giants Win," as two elderly Jewish men in old-fashioned dress gaze at him quizzically and indulgently. Their smiles indicate amusement that, in this new world, a game of baseball should be so important as to make big newspaper headlines.

ILLUSTRATORS AND ILLUSION

Newspapers and magazines were the primary sources of information and entertainment. Their illustrations, read as literally as the human interest stories and current events features to which they were related, often constituted the most potent pictorial record of an era. Magazines, in particular, were dependent upon the goodwill and largesse of both subscribers and newsstand patrons. With sales a major concern, covers were specifically designed to reflect the taste and attitudes of a mass audience. Baseball imagery was a guaranteed draw. By the teens and into the Twenties and Thirties, there was such a profusion of periodicals, all competing for the same market, that illustrators and their familiar themes were at a premium.

Joseph Christian Leyendecker (1874–1951) had studied fine art at the Art Institute of Chicago and the Academie Julian in Paris. He was a much-sought-after magazine illustrator whose works graced countless covers of popular magazines, including *Collier's* and the *Saturday Evening Post*. His painting "Baseball Scene of Batter, Catcher and Umpire," reproduced as a *Collier's* cover on October 9, 1915 [Fig. 32], is a forthright pictorial representation, without nuance. The batter's posture is almost lackadaisical as he patiently awaits the pitch. His intent, disarming gaze engages the unseen pitcher—and the reader—with an expression bordering on contempt. The faces of the catcher and umpire, behind their masks, are properly solemn and watchful. There is no backdrop of screaming fans or bright-color highlights to accentuate the scene. Nothing is presented that would interfere with direct communication. The painting was

30. Thomas Fogarty, *The Town Team*, c. 1905

31. Maurice Sievan, *Newsboy*, 1914

42

32. Joseph Christian Leyendecker, *Baseball Scene of Batter, Catcher and Umpire*, 1915

obviously commissioned for the purpose it so effectively serves.

Ten years later, another prominent illustrator, Frank Hoffman (1888–1958), was able to present a painting in motion. Reproduced as a *Liberty* magazine cover on April 18, 1925, "Safe at Home" [Fig. 29] shows a redheaded disheveled player, kicking up the dust, sliding directly into the catcher's protective stance. The umpire, face mask in hand, is preparing to make the call. There is nothing subtle about the sharp color or the vivid action portrayed. The public's needs and expectations had quite evidently changed.

Three-dimensional figures, however, continued to rely on classicism retaining the heroic proportions, the balance and weight of their antecedents. Oronzo Cosentino's (n.d.) bronze sculpture "Baseball Player (First Baseman)" (c. 1915) [Fig. 35] is a strong, purposeful, carefully modeled figure. The sweep from waist through outstretched arms, the tense posture and resolute facial expression attest to an aggressive first baseman's determination to complete the play successfully.

Although paintings of black ball players and spectators were rare, an unknown artist ventured a beautifully constructed naive painting of an all-black ball team in the midst of a suspenseful action [Fig. 34]. The pitcher is into his windup, the batter is up, expectant. A player wanders down the base path from first to second, while his teammate stands patiently on third waiting for the pitch to come down. Two elegantly dressed women watch intently from the sidelines. On the bench all eyes are highlighted, concentrating on the batter. The artist is obviously not conversant with traditional composition and technique, yet the painting manages to convey its own energy in an informal context. Although the title, painter, and date are unknown, the numbered jerseys would indicate a 1920s time frame; the women's clothing, however, is of an earlier vintage.

DISILLUSION:
THE CHICAGO BLACK SOX SCANDAL

While many artists were confronting the hard facts and the crude, often humorous, elements of the burgeoning urban society, baseball, with its two leagues now intact, was fast becoming a very big business indeed. Large parks were being built and franchises expanded. A livelier ball was introduced which gave the batter at least equal status with the pitcher's established machinations. Competition was keen, and

33. George Bellows, *Take Him Out*, 1906

44

the wild, improbable hold the game had on its legions of fans grew stronger and more intense. Players attained the status of folk heroes. The better they performed, the more attention they received; the more they were paid, the greater the satisfaction, or so it seemed . . . until the scandal broke.

When eight players on the Chicago team, known forevermore as the Chicago Black Sox, threw the World Series in 1919, the world of baseball reacted with confu-

sion and panic. The public trust had been defiled as never before and shock waves threatened destruction. Although the game's dishonor represented profound financial distress for the owners, it was the public's perception of the joyous summer spectacle which suffered most the breach of trust. Self-interest ultimately prevailed, however, and, although tried and acquitted of conspiracy, the infamous players were removed from all professional contact with

34. Unidentified Artist, *Untitled (Black Baseball Players)*, n.d.

the sport. As a direct result of the scandal, a commissioner-overseer, the autocratic Judge Kenesaw Mountain Landis, was appointed in perpetuity and given broad absolute power. The game went enthusiastically forward once again. Commissioner Landis remained the single, most visible standard-bearer of baseball's incorruptibility until his death in 1945.

The 1920s were alive with prosperity and good feeling. It was bathtub gin time, with gaiety and careless play. Life was an eternal merry-go-round and baseball reaped the benefits. Multitudes crowded the steel and concrete stadiums, gate receipts soared, everyone wanted to have fun, and whatever the residue left by the Black Sox scandal, it was more than ameliorated by the advent of a great slugger, the larger-than-life George Herman (Babe) Ruth. He set astounding records with impunity, almost without trying. He was the exact image of the age and the game. When Yankee Stadium was completed in 1923, it was truly the "House That Ruth Built." Other player-heroes have moved in and out of the nation's consciousness, still others have eventually broken some of his records, but Ruth remains the inviolable symbol of the game. Nickolas Muray (1892-1965) presented him in an unusually contemplative studio portrait "Babe Ruth (George Herman Ruth)" (1927) [Fig. 24].

35. Oronzo Cosentino, *Baseball Player (First Baseman)*, c. 1915

36. James Daugherty, *Three Base Hit*, 1914

JAMES DAUGHERTY

THE FUTURIST EXPLOSION AND AN EXULTANT MODERNISM

As the twentieth century progressed, the sudden expansion of metropolises, the unexpected huge growth in population and environmental changes, all strained the livability of urban areas. Buildings rose to unreasonable heights, darkening the narrowed streets; images of open spaces and broad vistas disappeared into the vast, sprawling, unplanned urban scene. The speed, the anxiety, the sheer nervous energy of the machine age became dominant elements. The incursions of European trends on the American aesthetic persisted, with modernists vying with the established realists for primacy.

James Daugherty (1890–1974) was clearly influenced by the Italian Futurist painters who captured the exploding, chaotic anarchistic quality of the city in whirling fragments and colors. Using the distorted forms from these mad, surging cityscapes, he created his own Futurist emblem, "Three Base Hit" (1914) [Fig. 36]. It was reproduced in the *New York Herald* on April 12, 1914, as "Futurist Picture of the Opening Game" with the following analysis by the artist: "...This is not a picture of a baseball game. It is a representation of the various sensations of the onlooker. The pitcher whirls about, a confusion of head, arms and legs. The ball flashes across the diamond in curves that make a snake look like a curtain rod. The batter swings the stick in flashing semi-circles, driving the ball like a comet over the first baseman's reach into the field. The runners tear around the diamond in a hurricane of flying legs and arms. The ball comes skyrocketing back from the field to the third baseman's mitt as he fails to block a famous slide. One side of the grand stand is a crazy quilt of waving hats and yelling mouths; on the other side the fans present a checkerboard of gloom—the losing bets..." The triangular images in the stands are abstracted, but the vigor and boundless energy of the players spring from the canvas with an almost frightening intensity. Daugherty used baseball to make an aesthetic judgment and it immediately became a popular newspaper illustration. He exerted an artist's prerogative by detailing a stylistic preference, but it was the game of baseball which made his point instantly accepted.

There was an exultant optimism to modernist experimentation, a desire to finally break the bonds of tradition, to transfer the eccentricities of city life to canvas in non-

37. John Marin, *Baseball*, 1953

38. Vaclav Vytlacil, *Baseball Player*, 1932

objective terms. In 1921 Vaclav Vytlacil (1892–1984), a native New Yorker, followed the time-worn path to Paris and then to Munich, where he remained for four years as a student of the innovator of non-objective art, Hans Hofmann. Vytlacil incorporated the harsh garish colors of the German expressionists into flattened modernist conceptions. His "Baseball Player" (1932) [Fig. 38] projects an impersonal vision. The featureless batter assumes a crouching stance, holding the bat high, the

catcher a mere smudge behind him. The stands are crowded with simple oblongs, the figures in the nearer boxes only slightly more distinct. This generates a strong visceral excitement, without the added ease of identification.

American modernism meant diversity, highly individual styles based on personal insights and the conscious determination to be independent of traditional values. All of these tenets are exemplified in the dynamic imagery and staccato lines of John Marin's

(1870–1953) continuing homage to urban New York and rural Maine. Marin was a master of watercolor. His work in this medium has a light, airy translucency expressive of a lively, witty, totally irreverent viewpoint. His buildings might tilt somewhat haphazardly, his boats might hug the crest of the wave, but they are never without support. His vistas are encapsulated, engulfed in patterns and designs, but always recognizeable and inviting. Marin's vision remained constant

39. John Sloan, *Design for New Mexico Baseball Team Uniforms*, c. 1926

for five decades. His color crayon and pencil drawing "Baseball" (1953) [Fig. 37] was completed the year he died. It depicts an elongated figure sliding desperately toward home plate. He is tagged unceremoniously while the umpire stands immobile just beyond. Perhaps he is safe; perhaps not. The outcome appears besides the point; it is the sheer audacity of the play that stimulates the excitement surrounding it.

Although the floodgates had barely opened, the slow but steady flow of population from crowded Eastern cities to the expansive Southwestern plains was beginning. In addition to technological and industrial growth, it brought, as might be expected, an increased and excited interest in team sports and baseball, in particular.

John Sloan (1871–1951), a founder of the Ashcan School who was best known for his dramatic settings and humorous invocations of city life, established an art colony outpost, in conjunction with other artists, in provincial Santa Fe, New Mexico. Removed from the literal stimulation of New York City, he reverted to model studies and romantic imagery, incorporating the odd orange-red light of the Southwest into his paintings. He was so intrigued by the customs and dress of his new environment, however, that he recreated a baseball player wearing an amusing, but hardly fitting, amalgam of gaucho costume and regulation uniform in his simple drawing "Design for New Mexico Baseball Team Uniforms" (1926) [Fig. 39].

40. William Zorach, *Baseball Player*, 1940

Part Three

The stock market disintegrated in 1929, bringing to a sudden, shuddering halt the growth and vitality of the much-heralded Industrial Age. The flimsy naive optimism of a giddy era simply evaporated, leaving in its wake a primitive struggle for survival. It was a tumultuous, anarchistic time, rife with critical worldwide political and financial problems apparently without solutions, bringing into question the very validity and integrity of government. Creative concepts emerged, however, despite the usual bureaucratic entanglements, when the newly elected President, Franklin Delano Roosevelt, set in motion a series of economic and social reforms, and with them the daring cultural experiments of the New Deal.

Artists, in concert with many others, had been set adrift, left destitute, without recourse to their customary private patronage or useful employment. The government channeled its subsidies to them through relief agencies such as the Public Works Administration (1933), the Treasury Department's program for the decoration of public buildings, called the Section of Fine Arts (1934), and, most effectively, through the Federal Arts Project of the Works Progress Administration, which lasted from 1935 to 1943. These projects not only provided the necessary financial relief for individual artists, they also attempted to make art a stronger, more recognizable factor in American daily life and, thereby, to improve the quality of that life.

Murals were designed and executed in public buildings throughout the country. Artists presented their studies to regional councils in competition. Although realism in all its aspects prevailed, there were areas allotted to abstract artists as well. Mural art was only one phase of the total production. There were also easel paintings, sculpture, prints, photographs, and an Index of American Design which heralded the importance of American folk art. As the government responded to their needs, artists produced an inventory of extraordinary proportions. Development of public understanding and appetite for the arts soon became a national concern. With active participation in the decision-making process and interchange of ideas came confrontation and conflicting aesthetic and social points of view. The visual arts were finally available for discussion, out in the open market, a viable cultural option—and free.

Content and style were as diverse as the artists themselves, and as contradictory as the time. Whether criticized or praised, the

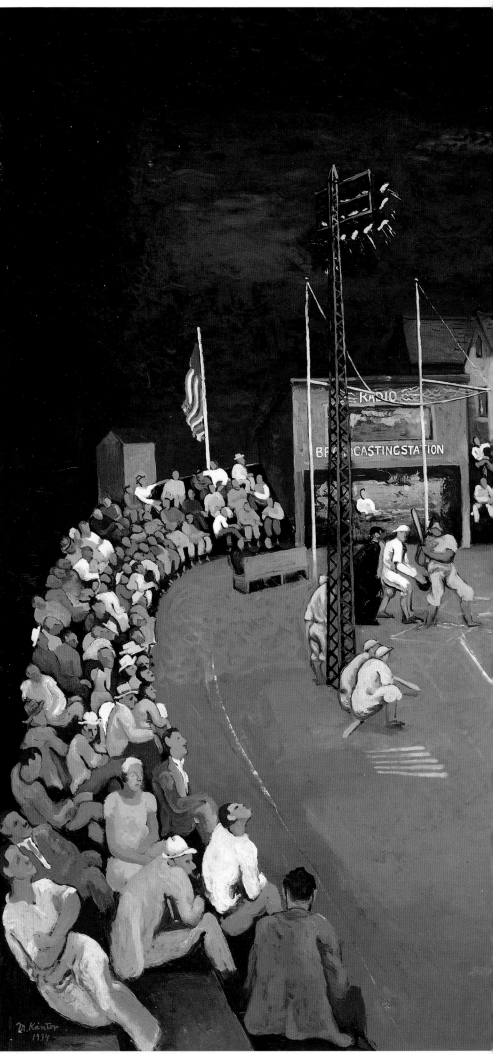

41. Morris Kantor, *Baseball at Night*, 1934

42. Arnold Friedman, *World Series*, n.d.

subject was the American scene and the styles were reflective of its imagery. There were the social realists, who presented their work as information, as propaganda, as anger, and as frustration at a world in disarray; the magic realists, whose images were a symbolic enactment of hunger, loneliness, isolation, and thwarted rebellion; the romantic realists, who continued to relate art to nature; and the realists, who remorselessly depicted the environment exactly as it was. They battled for primacy

58

in meeting halls, in publications, and one on one. They were all revolutionaries, although some would heatedly dispute that contention, in that they placed their aesthetic and stylistic concerns in the forefront of public opinion, eager for approbation. Elitism, in the arts at least, had disappeared into a dream of an egalitarian society. But then World War II exploded and violence more profound and unrelenting than ever imagined totally absorbed the United States and the rest of the world.

SEPARATING THE MEN FROM THE BOYS: SANDLOT COMPETITION TO PROFESSIONAL CONTESTS

In the midst of the economic disaster and depression of the 1930s, baseball persisted, as much an escape valve as entertainment. Where once English milkmaids had ingeniously placed stools as bases on sunny grassy knolls in the eighteenth-century game of rounders, the streetwise kids of the twentieth century set up tin cans.

43. Henry Ives Cobb, *Back Lot Baseball*, c. 1930s

44. Philip Evergood, *Early Youth of Babe Ruth*, c. 1939

Baseball was the great leveler. Whether its fans climbed to the heights of the bleachers or sat in the boxes at third base, their loud, raucous voices sounded from every vantage point; rooting for the team was the unifying factor. Stickball drew upon its own vocal viewers, their lusty calls echoed from window ledges to the crowded perimeters of the makeshift diamonds.

Artists, though intent on their perceived political differences, succumbed as well. They understood that baseball truly represented the American scene. They could see, just by attending a game, the hold it had on the general public. Baseball extolled the group dynamic while emphasizing the isolation of the individual, and all else aside, it was fun to participate and to portray.

In recognition of all these factors, the government built baseball parks and playgrounds as part of the public works projects and endowed them with the latest in technological innovations. Brightly lit night games and radio broadcasts, direct from booths in the parks, encountered stiff owner resistance at first; however, by the end of the decade, they were acknowledged as the means by which the game survived. Promotional stunts, gimmicks, and giveaways brought it to the attention of the very few people whose interests might possibly lie elsewhere. And then there were the great stars, the mythical heroes, the Babe Ruths, Dizzy Deans, and Lou Gehrigs who put their personal stamp on the game. The future was assured in August 1939, when the Brooklyn Dodgers/Cincinnati Reds game was telecast from Ebbets Field in Brooklyn, New York. Still, it wasn't until after the war that television was able to bring its extraordinary public outreach to the game.

SOCIAL REALISM AND THE AMERICAN SCENE

Artists quickly responded to the heightened excitement engendered by nighttime baseball's dramatic staging. The glare of artificial lights illuminating yet shadowing the playing field, sharply delineating the players themselves, added a new visual

Although bats of carefully determined uniform weight and length had become the important tools of the professional game, the kids found that broom handles served just as well. Stickball was improvisation, and the traffic-clogged streets, back alleys, and vacant lots became impromptu neighborhood playgrounds.

Just such a fenced-in, unkempt, rocky lot with clotheslines, filled with wash, swaying from nearby tenement windows provided the inspiration for Henry Ives

Cobb's (b. 1883–unknown) gouache "Back Lot Baseball" (c.1930s) [Fig. 43]. He depicts a cheerful sunny day; the neighborhood kids have already climbed the fence and set the game's baselines. Even the ugly refuse-laden garbage cans are washed out by the clear bright light. The batter, stick still in hand, has hit a long, long ball. The loaded bases are rapidly emptying. Way in the back, the small young outfielder is waiting fruitlessly, both arms up, poised for a catch. Everyone is in motion.

dimension to the tension of the game.

Morris Kantor's (1896–1974) "Baseball at Night" (1934) [Fig. 41] is clearly reflective of the regionalism of American Scene painting. The setting is emblematic of Small Town, U.S.A.: People out for an evening's entertainment, gathering together in support of the local minor-league team. The pitcher is the central focus, his body contorted in the rhythmical distortion of the windup. The batter is poised, the fielders and umpire in position. Everything is in preparation for the next movement. Concentration on the diamond is intense. Around the field, the audience appears casual, even relaxed, just sitting back on wooden benches and watching. It is a study suspended in time. Only the banks of lights and the clearly marked broadcasting booth show this as a newsworthy event.

Continuing the nineteenth-century plein air tradition, but in a twentieth-century vernacular, Arnold Friedman's (1879–1946) "World Series" (undated, acquired by the Phillips Collection in 1938) [Fig. 42] is played in a wide, airy space with few specifics, in direct contrast to Kantor's depiction. The breadth of the field provides an open vista. Although the stands are peripheral to the action in the park, the straw skimmers on the spectators reflect the aura of the afternoon sun, lightening the canvas perceptibly. Both of these works would seem to defy the aesthetic sensibility of the time. Rather than defining the human condition in apt socioeconomic terms, they simply demonstrate the people's capacity for infinite enjoyment even in the most difficult of times.

The social realists regarded American Scene painters with disdain, considering their work to be mere reproductions of untenable romantic visions, unrelated to the despair and dislocation of the Great Depression. In their view, the role of the artist was to reach out to the broadest audience possible, to influence its thinking and, thereby, to effect change. Their tools were satire, symbol, biting humor, and heroic imagery, and the game of baseball provided ample material.

Philip Evergood (1901–1973) was perhaps the most politically committed of the group. A gregarious, strongly opinionated man, he was a founding member and president of the radical Artist's Union and an active participant in the Artist's Congress of 1936. His work, however, is an amalgam of Surrealist invention and narration, peopled with oddly formed figures and usually overladen with detail, his line deliberately imprecise and wavering. Evergood was for-

45. Ben Shahn, *Vacant Lot*, 1939

mally trained at London's prestigious Slade School of Art, where he learned the meticulous drawing techniques practiced at the time. He studied at the Art Student's League with the Ashcan School's George Luks, returning to Paris several times for continued study. Because he was thoroughly grounded in the precepts of academic art, his primitivism in color and form, as well as the illustrational quality of his work, were certainly deliberate. "Early Youth of Babe Ruth" (1939) [Fig. 44], a narrative of the Babe's life in Baltimore, near Chesapeake Bay, presents an allegorical interpretation of the American dream of success. The two cartoonlike images of the Babe in the foreground, mitt and bat in hand, are enjoying a look back at lush farmland, amusement areas, and boats gliding through the blue waters of the bay. Quite a thematic departure for the socially relevant, often vitriolic, Evergood.

Ben Shahn (1898–1969), the quintessential exponent of social realism, had the unique ability to translate the prevalent attitudes toward social confrontation into a sensitive humanism. His references were pointedly topical, castigating the political excesses of the period in a visual language that was direct and understandable. An immigrant from Lithuania, he was eight years old when he arrived at Ellis Island and was already steeped in Biblical imagery and calligraphy. He had a broad sweep of stylistic concerns as a photographer, muralist, and graphic designer as well as a painter, often incorporating his camera studies into his paintings. Shahn was able to convey the utter loneliness of life in the impersonal poverty-ridden cities of the Depression. In "Vacant Lot" (1939) [Fig. 45] a small boy swings a bat as he walks slowly toward the corner of a rubble-strewn lot. A vast brick wall stretches endlessly before him. The center of the painting is empty of movement, of focus. The viewer's eye is forced to wander along with the tiny figure moving alone toward the edge of the painting. The joy of youthful play is paralyzed by the isolating environment. The painting has a quiet luminosity which envelops the solitary figure, removing him and his baseball bat from contact with the external world.

Sculptors were also involved in the

Works Progress Administration's Federal Art Project, producing architectural ornaments and figure studies for libraries, schools, and government buildings. William Zorach (1889–1966), along with the other art students of his generation, had studied painting in Paris, coming into contact with the new movements in French art, Fauvism and Cubism, and rejecting them, as had so many of his contemporaries. He turned to sculpture in the Twenties and remained, thereafter, a committed realist. Known primarily as a wood carver and stone cutter, Zorach was directed as much by the character of his materials as by his own aesthetic. His figures were heavy, blocked out, deliberately retaining surface evidence of hand carving. He preferred to master techniques, to develop and produce his work from conception to completion, without outside assistance. His interest in foundries and casting, therefore, was limited. The bronze "Baseball Player" (1940) [Fig. 40] was a departure for him, although its surface bears strong resemblance to the roughly hewn texture of his carvings. The catcher is in the appropriate kneeling position, with two fingers casually placed on the mitt as a signal to the pitcher. The details are precisely correct, from the body protector to the reversed cap. Solidly built, the squat figure is the confident guardian of home plate.

Even within the confines of social realism, artists found specific ways of injecting their own historical and personal perspectives into their works. Vivid colors and elegantly conceived figurative compositions forming semi-abstract patterns of design are the hallmarks of Jacob Lawrence's (b. 1917) inimitable style. Lawrence depicts the black urban experience with compassion and understanding. His narrative paintings define the essence of living in the ghettos of New York's Harlem and Bedford-Stuyvesant, at home, on the streets, in hospitals and playgrounds. Lawrence actually grew up in Harlem, studying at the Harlem Art Workshop, which was sponsored by the Works Progress Administration's Federal Art Project. He was subsequently employed by the W.P.A., where he came into contact with other artists of a similar point of view. He began his narrative series during the Depression and, in

46. Jacob Lawrence, *Strike*, 1949

47. Robert Riggs, *The Impossible Play*, 1949

48. Philip Evergood, *Come and Help Grandad*, 1944

49. Edward Laning, *Saturday Afternoon at Sportsman's Park*, 1944

1944, was the first black artist to have a retrospective at the Museum of Modern Art.

"Strike" (1949) [Fig. 46] was painted two years after Jackie Robinson joined the Brooklyn Dodgers and one year after the Cleveland Indians put on their roster the great, legendary pitcher Satchel Paige, at forty-two still a superstar in the Negro Leagues. Some thought that the signing of Paige was an adroit publicity stunt and it may well have been. Nevertheless, his remarkable pitching ability helped the Indians to their first pennant in twenty-eight years. There is a universality implicit in Lawrence's painting. The batter has swung wide of the mark; only his single visible eye mirrors his frustration. The ball is already in the catcher's mitt; the umpire has made his call and the next man up is kneeling in expectation. Vendors hawk their wares in the stands. The faces of the fans are featureless, but far from impassive. Their excitement is generated by the intricacy and boldness of the pictorial arrangement.

During the Depression, the game of baseball was also portrayed by artists whose works were unencumbered by political bias. Their concern was with the play itself, or with the grace and strength of the individual player. Nelson Rosenberg's (b. 1908) interest is in the overt depiction of speed. In "Out at Third" (undated, acquired by the Phillips Collection in 1939) [Fig. 50], the plumed flight of the ball spreads across the canvas. The third baseman's arm moves with a fluid elasticity, extending way beyond its actual reach, the mitt larger than life. He successfully makes the out, while just below, the sliding figure leaves in its wake a burst of sparkling white heat, but to no avail.

Just as Nelson Rosenberg's motivation had been the visual effect of an individual action, Louis Bouché's (1896–1969) interest, in virtually the same time frame, was the joy of the game itself. His "Baseball Game, Long Island" (1939) [Fig. 51] takes place in a leisure setting, an expansive grassy field just off the blue waters of the bay, idyllic in conception and deliberately reminiscent of an easier, more relaxed time. The figures, barely discernable, cavort about with a notable lack of serious intent. The only intrusion of reality is a partially decipherable sign on a distant building which could be translated as "Bay Building Materials."

50. Nelson Rosenberg, *Out at Third*, n.d.

ARTISTS DOCUMENT THE NATION AT WAR

The World War II years were chaotic and disruptive, a time of extreme personal anxiety tempered by a universal dedication. Patriotism was the bond, of course, and the war effort paramount. But it was an illogical era of dislocation. The very fabric of American society seemed irretrieveably altered. Able-bodied men enlisted eagerly or were drafted; women, who had been primarily homemakers, disappeared into the huge, expanding defense plants and factories. Only the elderly, the feeble, and the very young were visible. Baseball, as usual, reflected the times. Teenagers were playing professional ball and old-timers were brought out of retirement. They were caretakers, holding the game intact. Amazingly, attendance did not diminish precipitously. The need for entertainment was so evident that the viability of America's national pastime was never in question. In recognition of baseball's essential relationship to the national morale, President Roosevelt wrote to Commissioner Landis and informed him that the game would carry on to the fullest extent possible, in whatever manner was consistent with the nation's primary purpose of winning the war.

Artists were pressed into government service with everyone else. As foot soldiers, as observers, and as war correspondents, their job was to report on the fatigue of battle, the ghastly destruction, the unspeakable horrors of genocide, annihilation, and individual death. Whatever the theoretical and political discord that preceded the artists' involvement, it vanished in the real onslaught of a terrible war. The assignments were arduous, emotionally as well as physically disorienting. Reactions were subjective. There were those who could narrate the tales of war with descriptive violence and with seeming indifference. Others, more reflective, delved into their own peculiar psyches for individual responses, while some still retained a heightened sense of social purpose.

The dislocation of the relationship between young and old, the imposition of defense factories and their auxiliary services on the landscape, are the themes of Philip Evergood's sentimental painting "Come and Help Grandad" (1944) [Fig. 48]. A large factory complex dominates the center. On one side a boy in a baseball cap stands alone and disconsolate, bat and ball in hand; on the other, an elderly farm couple are desperately trying to scratch the surface of poor ground. They urgently require their grandson's youthful energy, though he remains apart, seeking the reassurance that life will return to a playtime of games in the summer sun. The underlying sadness is contradicted by Evergood's customary harsh discordant colors and hard lines.

Artist-correspondent Edward Laning (1908–1981) worked for *Life* magazine during the tempestuous war years of 1943 and 1944, recording with meticulous detail the grinding battles for supremacy on Italian terrain. Laning, who had actually started his career as a modernist, left Chicago's Art Institute to study with Max Weber at the Art Student's League in New York in 1926. While there, he came under the influence of John Sloan and Kenneth Hayes Miller, among others, and emerged an ardent advocate of the realist cause. An articulate, urbane man, Laning, with such other social activists as Isabel Bishop and Reginald Marsh, soon became an observer and recorder of the vibrant panorama of life around his West Fourteenth Street studio. The Fourteenth Street artists' concern for the economic and social inequities prevalent in the 1930s was fueled by the radical political activity, teeming tenements, honky-tonk atmosphere, and day-into-night streetlife of their immediate neighborhood. It was their window on the world.

After observing the great Mexican muralist Diego Rivera at work on the ill-starred murals for Rockefeller Center, later destroyed, Laning turned to urban mural painting, under the auspices of the Works Progress Administration's Federal Arts Project. His work remains in major public and corporate buildings, including the powerful four-part panel depicting the history of the printed word, which is on permanent display in the main branch of the New York Public Library. Although a master craftsman, Laning's conservative approach to art and his vehement opposition to change were inhibiting factors. His painting "Saturday Afternoon at Sportsman's Park" (1944) [Fig. 49] is a lesson in reportage well learned.

In 1944 the quality of baseball play was mediocre at best. The war was still gathering momentum, with the end not yet in sight. Emotions at home were at a fever pitch of anxiety and anticipation. If the games were

51. Louis Bouché, *Baseball Game, Long Island*, 1939

LOUIS BOUCHÉ 1939

52. Ferdinand E. Warren, *Night Ball Game*, 1946

53. Henry Koerner, *Rose Arbor*, 1947

not inspired, the fans certainly were. Baseball attendance was the highest since 1930. In this frantic atmosphere, the St. Louis Cardinals and the St. Louis Browns were battling for the first World Series championship to be played in its entirety west of the Mississippi River. The interest was intensified by the fact that this was the only time the Browns had won a pennant in their forty-three-year history. Sportsman's Park, owned by the Browns and leased to the Cardinals for their home games, was filled to the proverbial rafters with rapturous fans. Laning's painting expresses the intensity of their involvement. The viewer sits behind the wildly gesticulating fans, high in the bleachers, their disproportionately large figures almost obscuring the distant playing field; a vendor below, lost in this mad cacophony of sound and movement, laconically attempts to sell his bottles of beer. The painting is explicit in tone and accurate in detail, but, in its expressive quality, it was a departure for the customarily detached Laning.

Finally, the war was won. Relief and joy swept across the nation. Memories of loss and the scars remained, but a future could be acknowledged at last. The seasoned players and their professionalism returned to baseball. Gate receipts reached beyond the owners' wildest expectations.

The players, unfortunately, were not as financially fulfilled. When a rich, enterprising, Mexican entrepreneur decided to inaugurate a new Mexican League in 1946 and, in traditional baseball fashion, began to raid clubs, offering considerable salary advances, some players in the two major leagues jumped. Baseball Commissioner Happy Chandler, Judge Landis's successor, proceeded to outlaw the Mexican League and blacklisted the players for five years. As it turned out, the operation was slipshod and failed before it could cause serious damage to the organized game. After some legal maneuvering on the part of the returning players, the blacklist was rescinded and amnesty granted. Player discontent did not noticeably abate, however. In the spring of 1946, the American Baseball Guild was organized as a means of airing the players' grievances, which primarily concerned the lack of financial security. Strike threats were considered serious enough for Commissioner Chandler to hold meetings with player representatives. In order to head off a legitimate players' union, the owners agreed to a pension fund, a minimal annual salary of five thousand dollars, and an allowance for spring training. Within ten years, the Major

54. Seymour Leichman, *Fate Takes a Hand*, 1969

55. William Crawford, *Termites in the Temple*, c. 1946

League Baseball Players Association was formed, which became a powerful force in player-owner negotiations.

All of these machinations were brought to the public's attention by columnists and cartoonists. Baseball, after all, has always been big news. The *Newark Evening News* editorial cartoonist William Crawford (1913–1982) [Fig. 55], his bias biting and unmistakable, drew the national pastime as a bloated overpowering figure sitting clumsily astride a huge chair, while two small figures, identified as the Mexican League and the New Players' Union, desperately try to knock the pins (baseball bats) out from under him. The sardonic title, "Termites in the Temple" (1946), was particularly apt.

Change was in the air and a new strategy was inevitable. The limited acceptance of black players presaged the advent of a vast and avid audience which had remained largely untapped by the all-white ball clubs. The remarkable new media tool, television, was capable of spreading interest in the game to millions nationwide. And perhaps most important, the peacetime economy continued to surge forward. War production was transformed into consumer production with relative ease. It was a time for reevaluation, for the setting forth of new goals in art as in sports.

ABSTRACT IMPRESSIONISM, SYMBOLISM, AND SHARP-FOCUS REALISM

Abstract Expressionism, with its dynamic fields of color, new methods of paint application, visual intensity, and emotional involvement, broke the limiting boundaries of representational art. The vision was intensely personal and emotionally searching. The dilemma for many viewers was the lack of recognizable imagery. This essentially American movement swept through the art world, generating controversy and excitement. For some realists the ferment was reflected in changes in perspective, in the way they visualized their surroundings. Their concern for continuity necessitated the depiction of commonplace themes, but with less detail and greater introspection. Removing themselves from the raging debate over abstraction, they attempted to incorporate the past within new aesthetic dimensions. Other artists remained nonparticipants, choosing to view events dispassionately and from a distance.

Henry Koerner (b. 1915) emigrated from the depravity of Vienna in 1939, displaced by the horror of National Socialism. As

56. James Chapin, *Man on First*, 1948

an art student at the Vienna Academy of Design, he had absorbed the precise techniques of the Vienna School and the wide-ranging freedom of the German Expressionists. He arrived on the American shores with a comparatively few escapees who, like himself, were strangers, whose roots and real life remained elsewhere. When he returned to Europe under the auspices of the Office of Strategic Services in 1943 and 1945, it was to witness the ruins, the emptiness, the utter desolation which were the results of modern warfare. With his family gone, there was very little left for him in Vienna.

Koerner's paintings exemplify his sense of withdrawal and alienation. He projects himself as a remote observer, a nonparticipant, the existential loner. "Rose Arbor" (1947) [Fig. 53] depicts men and women acting out the play of two ball games, baseball and tennis. The figures intermingle, but never relate; each is engaged in a private activity. Across the arbor path, one solitary black youth is crouching, hands on knees, attentive, waiting for a ball. Koerner understands that baseball is in some respects a loner's game and that, ultimately, each player makes the tactical judgment and accepts the challenge alone. All the figures in the painting are immobilized, as if the separate images were photographed in place and carefully set to form a montage which intimated activity. Hidden within the circumference of the playing field and almost obscured by its textured surface, an embracing couple projects a tenuous link with warmth and affection. The lovely rose arbor with its trellis, bright flowers, and arched pathway is, at once, a shield and an enclosure. Viewers stand above and apart watching, while one, hands cupped to eyes, peers intently through the wire-mesh fence, an observer. Koerner presents no sign of joy in the games, only silence. His vision is almost surreal; he is the interpreter, the nonjudgmental onlooker.

James Chapin's (1887–1975) straightforward approach gives evidence that American Scene painters remained serious about direct imagery. As a student in Antwerp and Paris, Chapin had been profoundly influenced by the structural compositions of Cezanne and the modernists. He returned to New York imbued with the language and techniques of post-impressionism. His decision to leave the city for his home in rural New Jersey in 1924 meant a return as well to realistic portrayals of his neighbors and their workaday world, although he did retain some of the compo-

sitional elements and painterly values learned in his European sojourn. In his painting "Man on First" (1948), [Fig. 56] two singular figures are purposefully presented: the first baseman, stretches, awaiting the toss, his body stiff with tension and anticipation; the runner sidles slyly, and with some bravado, along the base path on the way to second base, if just given the opportunity. It's really a study of a game within a game, exactly as it is played.

For its sheer dexterity, for the image of man overcoming the odds, exciting his audience, and proving his ability, there is Robert Riggs's (1896–1970) evocation of "The Impossible Play" (1949) [Fig. 47]. The tension and strength of the foreground figures and the interaction of those on the field capture the essence of concerted motion as a vital play is initiated. The painting is clearly indicative of the dynamic visual impact baseball exerts on even a passive viewer. Riggs's vivid palette and narrow rectangular canvas, although well controlled, reveal a startling urgency.

Television, the soon-to-be media monster, had not as yet displaced the scores of large-circulation pictorial magazines devoted to all aspects of American life. Illustrators were still in great demand. Norman Rockwell (1894–1978), perhaps the most-sought-after illustrator of his generation, parlayed baseball's humorous byplays into many of his *Saturday Evening Post* magazine covers, spreading the game's largesse virtually everywhere. Rockwell's serious interest in art originally had led him to the academic confines of the National Academy of Design. Finding the atmosphere stuffy and inhibiting, he soon left for the comparative freedom of the Art Student's League. There, under the tutelage of Thomas Fogarty, he turned to the lighthearted evocations of everyday life which became his trademark.

His illustration for the September 4, 1948, issue of the *Post*, "The Dugout," [Fig. 57] describes, with understandable scorn, a particularly dismal period. The entire city of Chicago was in the cellar, as each of its two clubs, the National League's Cubs and the American League's White Sox, occupied last place, definitely out of the money. It had been a long and horrendous season. On this particular day, the players in the dugout are shown in total disarray, slumped and awkward, aghast at their own inadequacy, while the venomous faces of the fans form a background frieze of anger and frustration. He imparts his information with impeccable detail, tailoring it to the widest possible audience.

57. Norman Rockwell, *The Dugout*, 1948

58. Roy Lichtenstein, *Baseball Manager*, 1963

1950-1988:

Business
Plays Ball

Part Four

Big business caught up with baseball in the Fifties. Owners were acquiring teams much as they would companies and corporations. It was not so much for the sport as for the revenue. With television sending its signals over the entire land, baseball was no longer simply hometown teams playing to sometimes sparse hometown audiences. A national market was being created. Many of the established Eastern ballparks were becoming obsolete. They were located in densely populated, deteriorating inner-city areas where space was at a premium and expansion improbable. Franchise shifts were inevitable. The Boston Braves moved to Milwaukee in 1953, the St. Louis Browns to Baltimore in 1954, the Philadelphia Athletics to Kansas City in 1955. The sunshine and wide-open areas of the Far West and, especially, its fast-growing population offered seductive invitations that were eagerly accepted. The New York Giants moved to San Francisco in 1958, and then the unthinkable actually happened: The Brooklyn Dodgers, "Dem Bums," left for Los Angeles that very same year.

THE BROOKLYN DODGERS AND THE NEW YORK YANKEES

The powerhouse Fifties are epitomized by the blockbuster Brooklyn Dodger team and the formidable New York Yankees. The grandstanding, the heroics, and the despair of the four so-called Subway Series, as well as the remarkable ability of the players, remain chilling and exhilarating memories. It was the Dodgers' move, however, that was the most dispiriting. After years of laughter and ridicule, of erstwhile fans loyally staying in baseball's cellar with their team, of defying the pointed humor of writers and filmmakers, tunesmiths and comics, the Dodgers finally broke the bank, achieving four pennants in six years and, in 1955, winning a World Series, only to lose it all to the warm climate and cool attitudes of California.

Brooklyn had always been a baseball town. In the mid-nineteenth century, the city of Brooklyn's rural character, its hospitable green and open terrain, contributed to its focal position in the development of the national game. It spawned more than seventy teams by 1858, as compared to the mere twenty-five of its arch competitor across the East River, New York City. In the same year, the cities of Brooklyn and New York engaged in the first all-star game, a forerunner of the intra-city rivalries of the future.

59. Joseph Delaney, *Brooklyn Bums Clubhouse*, 1955

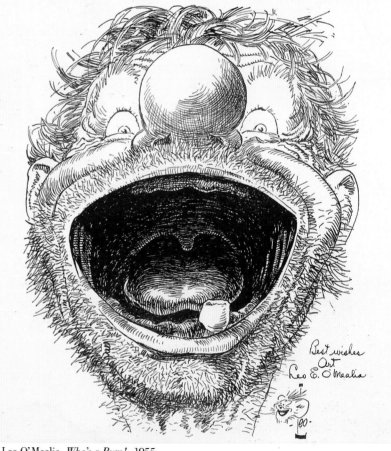

60. Leo O'Mealia, *Who's a Bum!*, 1955

61. David Levine, *Leo Durocher*, 1973

62. Willard Mullin, *Brooklyn Bum*, n.d.

Among Brooklyn's highly regarded teams of the time were the Excelsiors, the Atlantics, and the Eckfords. The Trolley Dodgers, named for those nimble, eager fans lucky enough to manage the maze of intersecting trolley car tracks and lines, became, successively, the Superbas, the Bridegrooms (identifying six stalwart teammates who married in 1889), the Robins, and, eventually, the Brooklyn Dodgers of song and legend. These teams were eclectic, fiercely competitive, hard playing, typically argumentative, and considerably removed from the original genteel elitists. The Excelsiors were the first officially organized club (1854), the first to go on tour (1860), and the first to pay, albeit surreptitiously, for the services of a preeminent player, James Creighton, thereby disproving the myth of amateurism.

Brooklyn's parks and playgrounds, its leisure activities, beaches, race tracks, and skating rinks, lured the fashionable sophisticates from New York. Out of season, however, many of these play areas with their large seating capacities accommodated the teams and the growing crowds of baseball enthusiasts. In 1913, Charles Ebbets successfully converted Pigstown, so-called because farmers brought their pigs there to feast on the squatters' fetid garbage, into the quintessential modern ballpark. A concrete and steel structure, Ebbets Field was situated in a confluence of urban traffic patterns. The subways, the elevated trains, the trolleys (horse and then electric) all eventually converged in Flatbush. Access was easy.

There were no class distinctions in Ebbets Field. The hoarse cries and catcalls were as one from the boxes and the bleachers; perhaps this was the lasting legacy of the game and its major impact on the people of Brooklyn. Although the city of Brooklyn joined New York in 1898, becoming one of five boroughs, it always retained its distinctive character, and that wonderful, daffy, dizzy team was its emblem. If the Dodgers won, the fans brought the house down; if they lost, it was "Wait till next year." The fans and the team they supported epitomized the tenacity and the strength of this volatile borough. The Brooklyn crowds were not merely attending an entertainment; they were the entertainment. The great Dodger Sym-phony, five loud musicians and a series of derisive songs; the ultimate fan, Hilda Chester, with her clanging cowbell; the delightful (as she was always called) Gladys Gooding at the organ, and Red Barber, the syrup-smooth Southern voice of Dodger radio—all have

63. Robert Weaver, *Ebbets Field*, 1981 (2)

passed beyond the local lore into the popular culture. This team of teams and its devoted fans sparked a joy in Flatbush in even the dreariest of times. The Dodgers may have been a business enterprise to Walter O'Malley, who heartlessly moved them away, and an idiosyncrasy to Robert Moses, who refused to allow land for a new stadium, but they were literally the breath and the beat of Brooklyn.

The interest in the Brooklyn Dodgers has never really abated. Since they left, books have been written and history rewritten. Baseball fans who never saw a game repeat their fathers' tales of the team's exploits. Politicians describe their loss in choice rhetoric. Songs are composed and media events occur. A special Brooklyn

Dodger Hall of Fame has been designated in a junior high school named for Jackie Robinson, and a determined group of Brooklyn citizens continues to plan for a new stadium and a new team.

The Dodgers were painted and drawn, illustrated, caricatured, and photographed. They symbolized the underdog overcoming great odds and achieving the farthest dream, the "Bums" making it, after all. The New York Yankees may have been considered aristocracy, but the Brooklyn Dodgers were everyman.

Their logo was Willard Mullin's (1902–1978) jaunty unshaven "Brooklyn Bum" (n.d.) [Fig. 62], down on his luck, with ragged clothing and half-shod feet, but, nevertheless, cheerfully swinging a bat and

64. Seymour Chwast, *The Grand Game of Baseball...and The Brooklyn Dodgers*, 1987

flicking a cigar ash as he strode along. He was represented in newspapers and magazines everywhere. So when the Dodgers finally won the 1955 World Series and Leo O'Mealia's (1884–1960) hugely grinning bum filled the entire front page of the New York *Daily News*, with a banner headline reading WHO'S A BUM! [Fig. 60], there was instant recognition, providing the one or two people left in New York City who weren't aware with the information that the earth-shaking victory had taken place at last.

Ebbets Field made the *Saturday Evening Post*'s cover on April 23, 1949, in an illustration that has become a classic comic reflection of the game. In his "Study for 'Bottom of the Sixth,'" [Fig. 65] Norman Rockwell groups three umpires in the foreground of the playing field, one with his palm held straight out to catch a trickle of rainwater, and all gazing solemnly upward at a single cloud in an otherwise blue sky. They are sternly and judiciously assessing the raindrop index. While not exactly

based on scientific data, their judgment will ultimately prevail. Continuation of the game between the Brooklyn Dodgers and the Pittsburgh Pirates appears imminent. In the background the Dodger manager is euphoric. Obviously his team would have lost had the game been called. In fact, the Dodgers did win the National League pennant in 1949, only to suffer a humiliating defeat by the Yankees in the World Series.

For many artists, portrayals of the players and the excitement they generated were

65. Norman Rockwell, *Study for 'Bottom of the Sixth'*, c. 1940s

66. Elaine de Kooning, *Campy at the Plate*, 1953–1980

'53-'80 Edok

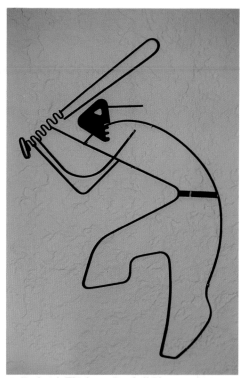

67. Frederick Weinberg, *Baseball Player*, c. 1950

68. Andy Jurinko, *Ebbets Field*, 1983

drawn from memories of childhood or from history. From Brooklyn-born Elaine de Kooning (1920–1989) to Brooklyn resident David Levine (b. 1926), from Lance Richbourg (b. 1938) to Andy Jurinko (b. 1939), remembered images, sometimes clouded by sentiment, sometimes excited by anger, sometimes just plain funny, are recorded on canvas, and on paper, to keep the "boys of summer" alive.

Elaine de Kooning did a quick study, probably on site, of "Campy at the Plate" in

1953 and returned to augment the painting in 1980 [Fig. 66]. Roy Campanella, Brooklyn's premier catcher and slugger, had undoubtedly hit a home run, as the glad-handed greeting he receives at the plate indicates, while a player with a large number six on his jersey, Carl Furillo, the great right-fielder, stands back waiting expectantly in the batter's box. The figures themselves are indeterminate, faceless, but the easy, open brushwork and splendid light enliven the image of a successful turn at bat.

David Levine, on the other hand, remembers himself as one with the throng in the bleachers in his painting of the "Crowd at Ebbets Field" (c. 1960) [Fig. 69]. It is an unusually dejected gathering of fans. The figures are presented in various postures of despair, signifying an expected Dodgers loss. The onlookers' concentration is intent on the field, and whether catcalling or quiet, they're carefully removed from one another. Lack of communication was not the customary

69. David Levine, *Crowd at Ebbets Field*, c. 1960

behavior pattern of Brooklyn's bleacher customers. Normally, the stands represented a social environment, a meeting place, an eating hall, a very loud discussion center. The artist has identified these fans individually and with understanding while emphasizing their special quality: total empathy with the players on the field. Levine, the caustic, incisive caricaturist, recollects Leo (The Lip) Durocher, the Dodgers' voluble, aggressive shortstop, then manager, who stood toe to toe with the umpires and, sometimes, nose to nose, in a delicious and cheerfully venomous pen and ink drawing (1973) [Fig. 61].

And then there are those artists who think of the history of an era, as in Lance Richbourg's "Jackie Robinson" (1988) [Fig. 70]. Robinson's strong stance is the focus: feet wide-spread, bat up high and to the right, his body rigid in expectation, awaiting the pitch. Does he connect . . .? It is the exact emotionally charged moment. This painter has an intimate sense of baseball, an almost tactile perception. The expertise and the excitement are with the player himself. Richbourg's shock of surrounding shades of red and mottled paint surface enhance the gritty drama of the scene, lending it an immediacy that belies the fact that more than thirty years have passed.

Using still another style, photo-realism, Andy Jurinko's "Dodger Lumber of '54" (1985) [Fig. 71] reproduces on canvas and in mammoth scale an original photograph of the power line-up: Gil Hodges (first base), Roy Campanella (catcher), Duke Snider (center field), and Carl Furillo (right field). They are kneeling, posed for the standard pregame picture. In the foreground are their crossed bats, a sign of camaraderie. They are relaxed as they smile benignly into the camera, effectively caught in the time warp of the Fifties.

The New York Yankees, on the other hand, inspired awe rather than love, envy rather than fealty. They were the superbly oiled machine, always in contention and with the funds available to acquire a disproportionate share of superstars. In the Twenties and Thirties, there had been the record makers, Babe Ruth and Lou Gehrig; a generation later, there were the record breakers, Mickey Mantle and Roger Maris. The American public virtually deified its old heroes, resisting the incursions on precious memories. But there was dedication and purpose to the goals of these younger men as well, and finally their compelling prowess and achievements entered the record books. Maris ultimately won the

70. Lance Richbourg, *Jackie Robinson*, 1988

71. Andy Jurinko, *Dodger Lumber of '54*, 1985

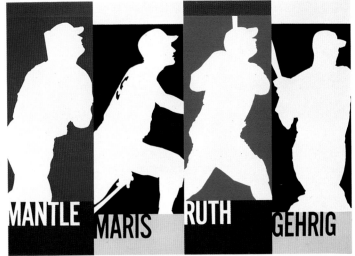

72. Kendall Shaw, *Four at Bat*, 1964

much-vaunted home run sweepstakes, happily removing the pressure and allowing the game itself to reassume its central role in the public's attention.

Sports columnists wrote endlessly about the Mickey Mantle-Roger Maris competition, just as they had written about the animosity between Babe Ruth and Lou Gehrig years before. Feature stories followed every game, and photographers, strategically placed, thrust their cameras forward with each pitch. Players in their prime make such good copy. Kendall Shaw (b. 1924) clipped ordinary newspaper prints and projected them in heroic human scale, flat across the picture plane, for his painting "Four at Bat" (1964) [Fig. 72]. Intense color contrasts shape the images. Mantle, Maris, Ruth, Gehrig, their names spelled out at their feet, are huge, impersonal cutouts in a formidable line-up of New York Yankee batting power, separated only by time.

Charles Dillon (Casey) Stengel, who managed the Yankees from 1949 to 1960, led the team to ten pennants. With his fractured English and rambunctious manner, Stengel provided the entertainment and the savvy. He was an astute manager and added a touch of human frailty to the seemingly invincible team. The Yankee brass, typically businesslike and without sentiment, turned him out unceremoniously in 1960 when the team failed to win the World Series. Casey's tangled quotes, dubbed "Stengelese" by sportswriters and their readers, was a boon to caricaturists as well. Illustrator Al Hirschfeld (b. 1903) lampoons a voluble Casey Stengel, secure in his own proper usage of the English language and determined to present his case, in a familiar ascerbic commentary. His ink

73. Al Hirschfeld, *Casey Stengel Teaches Samuel Johnson How to Speak*, c.1965

74. Justin McCarthy, *World Series, 1952 New York Yankees vs. Brooklyn Dodgers*, 1952

drawing "Casey Stengel Teaches Samuel Johnson How to Speak" (c. 1965) [Fig. 73] speaks for itself. Casey's pugnacious, protective attitude while striding toward the pitcher's mound or just standing back considering the angles, his hands thrust deep in his back pockets, his weatherbeaten face jutting forward with an intent and often dissatisfied gaze could have easily aroused a portrait artist's inspiration. It did in 1965, five years after the Yankee organization had ended his tenure and three years after he donned a New York Mets uniform. Rhoda Sherbell (b. 1933) sculpted his image in plaster and later cast it in polychromed bronze. "Charles Dillon 'Casey' Stengel" (1981) [Fig. 75] is a remarkable evocation of a man who relentlessly pursued his consuming passion for the summer game. In tribute, the artist placed a baseball on the ground before him as a symbol of his service.

An upstart expansionist club, the Milwaukee Braves treated the august Yankees rather badly in the 1957 World Series. The move from Boston to the Midwest had resulted in the Braves attaining the highest attendance figures for a National League club that season, and they were pretty cocky about it. Their aggressive play was heightened by the fans' adulation and, surprisingly, they took the series in seven. The social realist painter Robert Gwathmey (1903–1988), in a departure from his customary Southern sociopolitical orientation, saw the game on October 4, 1957, and recorded the aftermath of the last out in explicit detail in his painting "County Stadium (World Series)" (1958) [Fig. 79]. The exuberance of the winning home team bounding out of the dugout, piling one upon the other in unrestrained joy, evokes the essence of comradeship, with the added promise of financial gain. In the forefront and in distinct contrast, a disconsolate New York player walks slowly off the field, reflecting the pain of the loss. Beyond the playing field the scoreboard tells it all — 1-0 MILWAUKEE — while below the usual statistics, the organization's grateful streamers spell out an important slogan, especially good for public relations: THANK YOU BRAVES BASEBALL FANS. For this team, it obviously paid to advertise.

AN INTERNATIONAL VIEWPOINT

That baseball imagery could achieve an international dimension is evident in the French Fauve painter Raoul Dufy's (1877–1953) version of a "Ball Park — Boston" (1950) [Fig. 78]. Dufy came to Boston in

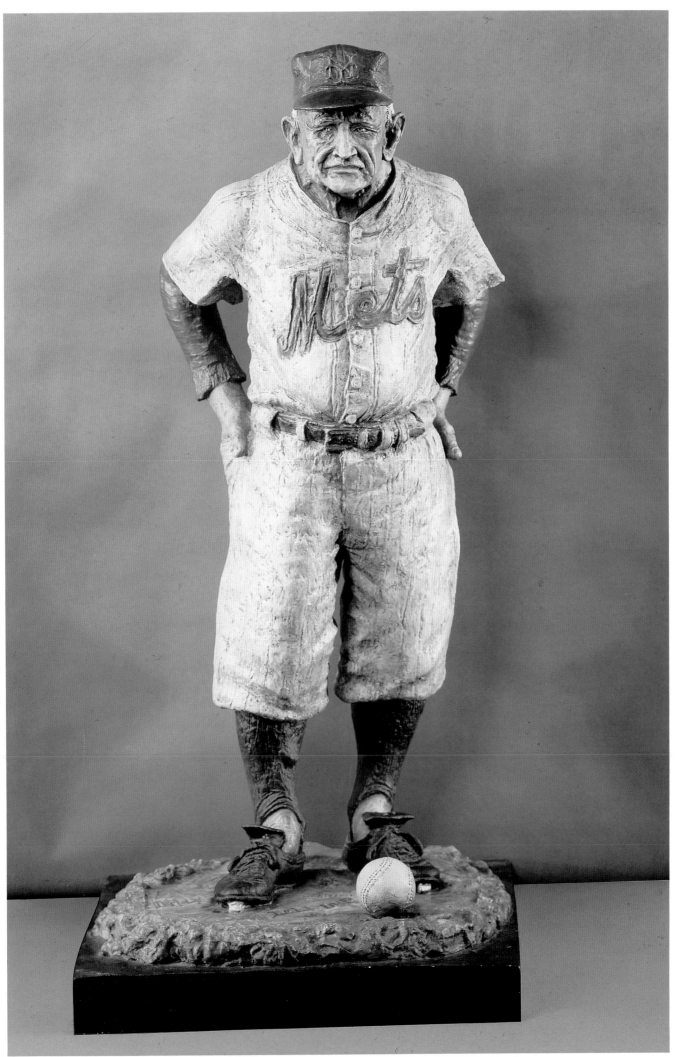

75. Rhoda Sherbell, *Charles Dillon (Casey) Stengel*, 1981

76. Norman Rockwell, *The Rookie*, 1957

1950 for treatment of a severely debilitating arthritic condition that had kept him in a wheelchair for many years. His hosts apparently decided that a warm welcome included a visit to a Boston Red Sox game, and his response was a typically detached Dufy product. Dufy had always been interested in technical as well as aesthetic diversity; he was an influential fabric designer, ceramicist, and illustrator. In his later years, however, his best-known works were of French sporting events, racetrack scenes, yacht races, and regattas, with their elegant, upper-class French audiences, hardly the stuff that Red Sox fans were made of. Dufy's distinctive broad planes of color, the bright green turf and muted blue sky, his remote and somewhat enigmatic style translate easily into this rather cryptic view of baseball. The simple, sketchy outlines of the players are almost engulfed in the expansive field. The pitcher is well into his windup, the batter is poised, the black-suited umpire, arm raised, is ready for the call. The banks of lights rise high above the ballpark, while below, in sharp contrast, bright bands of color, standing out in bold relief, identify the scoreboard and advertising signs. The audience is presented as an abstracted massing of brushstrokes and dots, simply a decorative adjunct to the whole. Dufy was a celebrator of the events he recorded. Clearly he understood and enjoyed the mechanics of the game and created this unique baseball painting as a testimonial.

THE SIXTIES ERUPT

The cataclysmic events of the next two decades altered the perception of the American dream and individual satisfaction with national goals. The brutal assassinations of a popular young President, John F. Kennedy, and a charismatic civil rights leader, Martin Luther King, the political chaos created by an unpopular war, the prevalent potentially explosive drug culture and its invasion of the world of sports—these were the hard realities confronting American society.

At the same time industrial expansion and economic growth were statistically evident and baseball's big-money moguls were in the forefront of financial success. New teams were organized for the first time since the advent of the American League in 1901, and both the National and American Leagues expanded their game schedules to 162 games. There was legitimate concern that the so-called expansion teams would not measure up to their well-entrenched

77. John Kennard, *Batting Coach, Little Falls, N.Y.,* 1983

78. Raoul Dufy, *Ball Park—Boston*, c. 1950

79. Robert Gwathmey, *County Stadium (World Series)*, 1958

opposition. However, the Minnesota Twins arrived in Minneapolis in 1961 and four years later were in first place. The Angels came to Los Angeles that same year and became the California Angels in 1966. New York finally acquired a franchise in 1962 and saw the birth of the Mets. That first year, under the guidance of the irascible Casey Stengel, they lost a total of 120 games, thereby fueling the pundits' meager expectations. Casey managed them for four more years. By 1969, however, the "Miracle Mets" confounded the experts and won the world championship. Their manager at that time was the old Brooklyn Dodger first baseman Gil Hodges.

Concern that the additional teams would strain the financial resources already in place became irrelevant with attendance peaking and the television industry paying vast sums for the privilege of televising the games. Despite television's appeal to the homebound, spirited fans came out in droves for the very same reasons they always had: the sheer enjoyment of direct visual and vocal communication and deep-rooted loyalty. And as each generation brought forward greater and more formidable heroes to cheer on to feats of glory, long-standing records of lifetime home runs, stolen bases, strikeouts, and games pitched, like those of Babe Ruth and Ty Cobb, were broken. New rules were composed to make the already knowledgeable spectator's enjoyment even greater. Pitching duels were considered exercises of

80. Marjorie Phillips, *Night Baseball*, 1951

intellectual virtuosity, but the fans still loved the excitement generated by the long ball hitter. "...The ball rebounds off the left-field wall...takes a short hop over the center fielder's outstretched glove...soars high into the bleachers...and listen to the crowd's roar..." —to quote the standard patter of a few breathless radio and television announcers.

By 1969, the pitching mound had been lowered from fifteen inches to ten inches and the strike zone reduced from shoulder-to-knee to armpit-to-top-of-knee. It obviously made a difference, for in that year the number of .300 hitters just about tripled. With continued expansion each league of twelve teams was divided into an eastern and western division; its championship was initially determined in a best-of-five play-off, which later was raised to seven. The anticipated complications and soothing public pronouncements never took place because so many of the fans, accommodating as usual, were able to develop new team or league loyalties. The understanding and acceptance of the game itself superceded personal identification with a specific team or player. Meanwhile, the summer season was further lengthened into the chills of autumn.

Dramatic changes in baseball's structure continued into the Seventies. The reserve clause, instituted in 1879 to insure the player's fidelity to the team, was demolished. No longer could the owners buy and sell their players' services at will. The con-

81. Tim Woodman, *Practice*, 1988

82. John Fawsett, *My Favorite Artist—Steinberg*, 1986

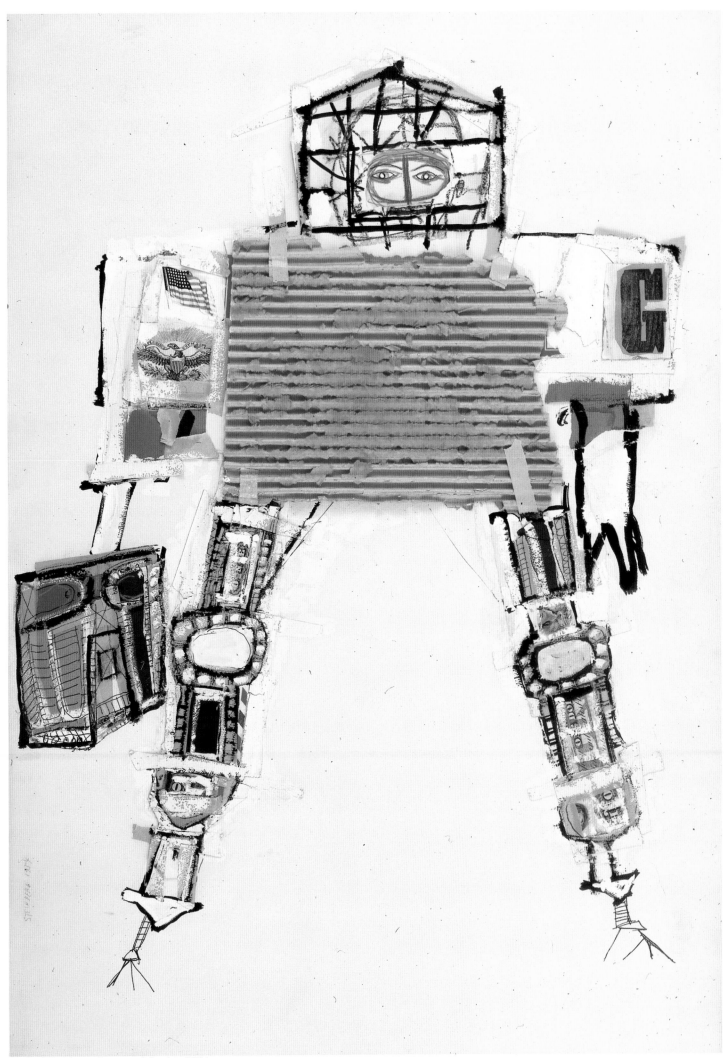

83. Saul Steinberg, *Corrugated Catcher*, 1954

cept of free agency emerged, and while salaries soared, so did profits. As usual, prognoses of the game's demise were greatly exaggerated. Partisan interest grew even stronger out-of-season as the clubs competed for players' services, with very hard bargaining and salary inducements, all open to public scrutiny. The superstar mentality was rampant. The media, naturally attentive to appearances, encouraged the reassessment of traditional dress codes. Suddenly uniforms were more ornate, and facial hair, mustaches, and beards, the ornaments of rebellion, were in vogue.

ART TAKES A COMIC-STRIP TURN

The Sixties was a decade of contrasts. An unpopular war precipitated controversy and anger, even while the concentration on material values persisted. Excess and availability were the by-words. Everything was larger than life-size. Cars, buildings, discotheques, extravaganzas, and Day-Glo colors were everywhere. This was the atmosphere that provided the basis for an art movement, originally English, that maintained a detached, uncritical view of the American environment. Named for populist attitudes, it was dubbed Pop Art. Its premise was simply that what was there objectively was important and what wasn't there did not exist. Everyday objects achieved a new monumentality: beer cans and hamburgers, lipstick holders, baseball bats and balls. Narrative comic strips, with their banal visual clichés, were reproduced intact, mechanically dotted and screened. It was art out of mundane matter, but cool and elegant. It was inevitable, therefore, that the artifacts and images of the American national pastime would be worthy of inclusion.

Although the new movement could not be contained, it was by no means untainted by controversy. Abstract Expressionism's continuing exposure of emotional angst had just about lost its spontaneous edge and was rapidly becoming a derivitive tale twice-told; nevertheless, it had its champions. The untidy forces of artist rebellion gathered in defiance, angry meetings were held, vituperative articles written; the lines were drawn. The influential, entrenched art establishment responded with derision and ridicule, but the excitement of experimentation was not to be denied.

Robert Rauschenberg (b. 1925) was an integral part of this period of change. Although the strong, undisciplined brush-strokes of Abstract Expressionism still dominated his picture planes, he began incorporating on their surfaces recognizeable objects and images of everyday life: photographs, picture postcards, even household junk. It was an outreach for a broader base of understanding. His "Canto XXIX: Illustration for Dante's 'Inferno'" (1959–60), [Fig. 84] one of a series, is a photomontage of images long held in memory. In the labyrinth are projected the dim outlines of naked bodies, disembodied faces, and implements of destruction. The contrasting images, most clearly defined, are those of an umpire standing resolutely behind the mesh screen, and a single baseball in a corner.

Roy Lichtenstein (b. 1923) was the comic-strip man. Using a deceptively simple technique, he projected his favorite characters, reproducing the Ben Day dots with screening until he achieved a true newsprint image. As in the comics, descriptive language was contained in the white clouds floating above the figures. His painting "Baseball Manager" (1963) [Fig. 58] is clearly derivative of a newspaper picture. The strokes are bold and black. Heavy shadows establish the outline and the facial contours, while the Ben Day dots set the image flat on the canvas. The depersonalized manager in his baseball cap and jersey, his lips pulled back in a slight sneer, exudes the arrogant power of command. Although articulated without words, the message is immediately understood. The crisp compositional elements inherent in the picture give it weight; the sudden click of recognition provides the pleasure.

Pop artists considered their work to be in harmony with the environment, a reflection of the individual's daily experience. They attempted to rediscover objects that, while always visible, were not really seen, and to develop the proper medium to put their concepts on display.

Claes Oldenburg (b. 1929) was an active participant in this experimental process. Initially, he had soaked fabric in plaster, molded it into shape, and then painted it with vivid enamel. Sometimes he had the muslin or burlap sewn and then stuffed with foam rubber or other supportive materials. He created fun food and furniture and the general appurtenances of congenial living as vivid adjuncts to household function. Oldenburg had worked in magazine illustration and design and the design element remained constant. As his vision grew, he transformed ordinary objects into grand-scale freestanding sculpture based in improbable environments, imparting in the meantime a solidity to his own fantasy.

84. Robert Rauschenburg, *Canto XXIX: Illustration for Dante's 'Inferno',* 1959–60

His monumental public sculpture "Batcolumn", installed in Chicago, exemplifies that city's devotion to its baseball heritage. The "Maquette for Batcolumn" (1975) [Fig. 86] has its own firm stance; the bright red welded steel bat, elegantly webbed, makes a forthright if immoveable statement reflective of the strength of the game. His lithograph "Bat Spinning at the Speed of Light" (1975) [Fig. 85] presents not only an illustrious image of "Batcolumn"'s grandeur, but also conveys the excitement of the moving, twirling instrument of ball play.

The marketplace was the art palace of the Sixties, with merchandise piled like pyramidal sites, the visual come-ons of supermarket display. There were goodies galore, and all available for a price. The art of marketing was honed to perfection and its apostle was Andy Warhol (1928–1987). How well he understood and depicted the public's acquisitive lust, reproducing the trite objects of its desires, Campbell's soup cans, Brillo boxes, S&H stamps, with an uncompromising clarity. In an era of kitsch and contrivance, he repeated image after image of celebrity icons such as Marilyn Monroe, Jackie Kennedy, and Truman Capote, and of catastrophic events such as President Kennedy's assassination, horrendous car crashes, and death in the electric chair—all in a similar, monotonous, repetetive form which preempted the devastating consequences. Nothing was too foul or too pretty. When viewed chronologically, his paintings and prints, his movies

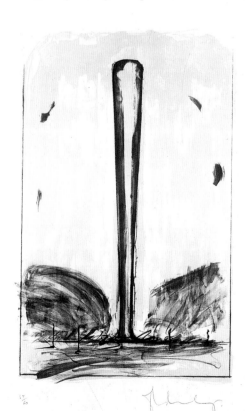

85. Claes Oldenburg, *Bat Spinning at the Speed of Light*, 1975

106

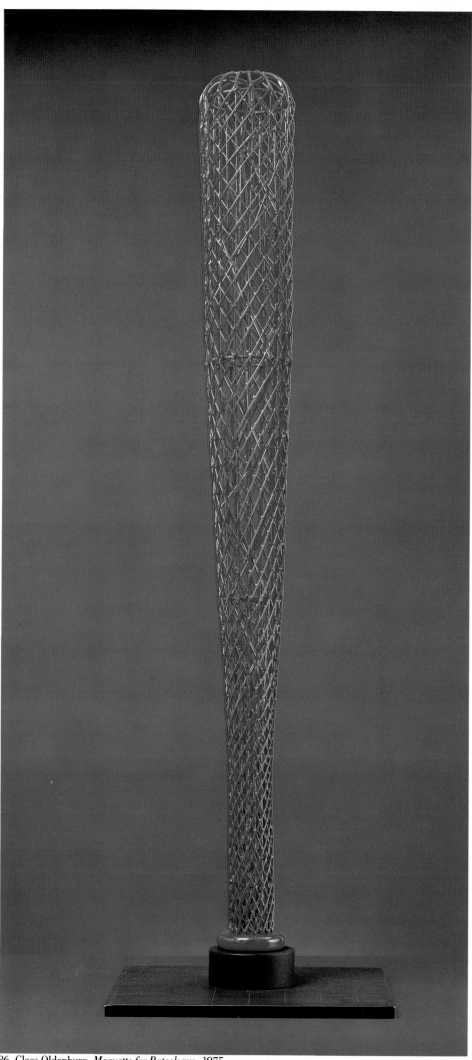

86. Claes Oldenburg, *Maquette for Batcolumn*, 1975

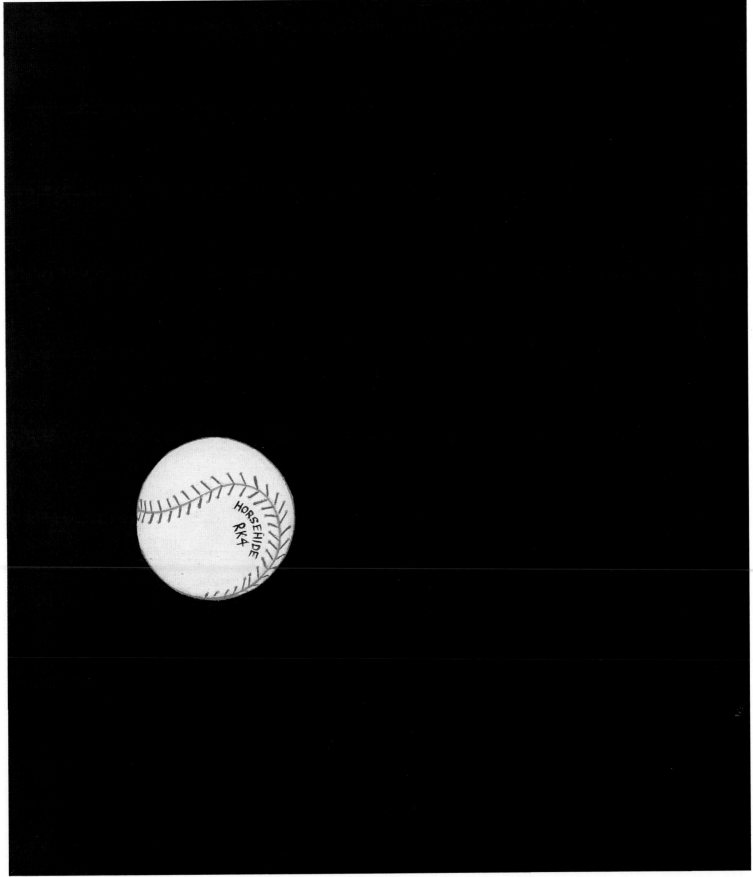

87. Ernest Trova, *Baseball*, c. 1960

88. Andy Warhol, *Baseball*, 1962

89. Leigh A. Wiener, *The Giant Killer*, 1963

and happenings, represent the narrative history of a unique age of excess.

Warhol's first silkscreen, "Baseball" (1962), [Fig. 88] repeats in a seemingly endless series, a grainy, blurred newspaper print depicting Roger Maris at bat. With deliberate intent, the surface has absorbed too much ink or too little, forcing one picture frame into the next. The figures are whole or slightly cropped. The effect is very much like the small children's books of illustrations which, when flipped, simulate movement. He projects an instantly recognizable image of an action in progress.

The carefully crafted baseball, pedestrian as it may seem, also deserves a place in the iconography of experience. Ernest Trova (b. 1927), whose forte was the polished brass "Falling Man" sculptures, placed a single brand-new unscuffed ball off center on a dead-black backdrop and let it hang in space for his painting "Baseball" (c. 1960) [Fig. 87]. Far from signifying isolation, it stands out as an object of force.

The new realism had a national appeal. Wayne Thiebaud (b. 1920), who lives and works in California, started his art life as a Disney Studio animator, cartoonist, and commercial art director, eventually translating his interest in layout and design into sharply defined, beautifully constructed images of sustenance: food and junk food. These pleasurable aspects of everyday life include cakes and pies, lollypops, gum drops, and cherries, among other less than nourishing staples. Baseball only adds to the pleasure. Thiebaud's "Hats" (1988) [Fig. 90] depicts those seemingly irrelevant uniform appendages, protective baseball caps. Painted in bright primary colors, some decorated with the symbolic crossed bats and ball and lined in row upon row of glistening patterns, they are accorded an exceptional presence.

Preceding the pop art movement in New York, London's Royal College of Art produced a group of young artists who were actively exploring the material aspects of English society. They projected multiple images, affixing real, everyday objects and explanatory writing, densely filling the canvas. It was a casual juxtaposition of the artifacts and fantasies of their own existence. Their vision was directed toward mass communication, a recapitulation of the known.

R. B. Kitaj (b. 1932), an American studying at the Royal College on the G.I. Bill, played an influential role in the development of this erratic movement. Kitaj toyed with the picture plane, going beyond the boundaries, transmitting successive

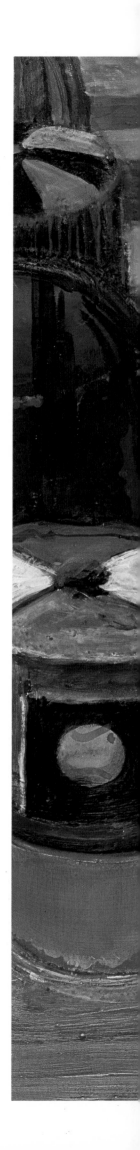

90. Wayne Thiebaud, *Hats*, 1988

91. Richard Merkin, *Kirby Higbe (22-9), Whit Wyatt (22-10) and the Pitching Staff of the National League Champion Brooklyn Dodgers, 1941, Minus Tamulis*, 1967

images, often unrelated, in order to create a visual paradox. He moved on from the recognizable to the abstract, interested in the feeling and texture of the painted surface. He created puzzles for the viewer to solve. "Upon Never Having Seen Koufax Pitch" (1967) [Fig. 92] is essentially a color field painting with only a small square attached containing the words of the title. That stationary field utterly devoid of movement states a sad, undeniable truth because, in fact, Sandy Koufax, the boy from Brooklyn, the great Los Angeles Dodger pitcher, played his last season in 1966 and would not pitch again. Koufax, who was elected to baseball's Hall of Fame after only twelve seasons in the major leagues, was a quiet hero, going about his pitching duties with incredible dexterity and aplomb. Leigh A. Wiener (b. 1929) caught Koufax's dynamic tension in the split second before the pitch for his black-and-white photograph "The Giant Killer" (1963). [Fig. 89]

Directly related to Kitaj and the English pop artists' penchant for assemblage and nontraditional spatial relationships, Richard Merkin (b. 1938), an iconoclastic painter and writer, concentrates on the development of single themes through seemingly unrelated references: photographs, portraits, history, language. Merkin draws upon a wellspring of information and, although he tries hard to compress his imagery, it spills out and over huge canvases. "Kirby Higbe (22–9), Whit Wyatt (22–10) and the Pitching Staff of the National League Champion Brooklyn Dodgers, 1941 Minus Tamulis" (1967) [Fig. 91] is a mixed-media painting of grand design and comprehensive title. The artist's resolve is to cover an entire spectrum, reinforced by the unlimited factual resources at his command. In addition to Higbe and Wyatt, Merkin depicts the infamous "backstop," Mickey Owen, whose dropped pitch enabled the New York Yankees to win the 1941 World Series. He incorporates such diverse images as a cameo portrait of third baseman Riggs and a baseball with LARRY, for MacPhail, the general manager, clearly inscribed on it. He writes about Gladys Gooding and her rendition of the national anthem and enumerates the 1941 pitching line-up. There are topographical allusions as well: to spring training amid the palm trees on the baseball-crazy island of Cuba, to the lake in Brooklyn's Prospect Park, and to Flatbush and Bedford Avenues. The data is all there in a clear and unmistakable history, and

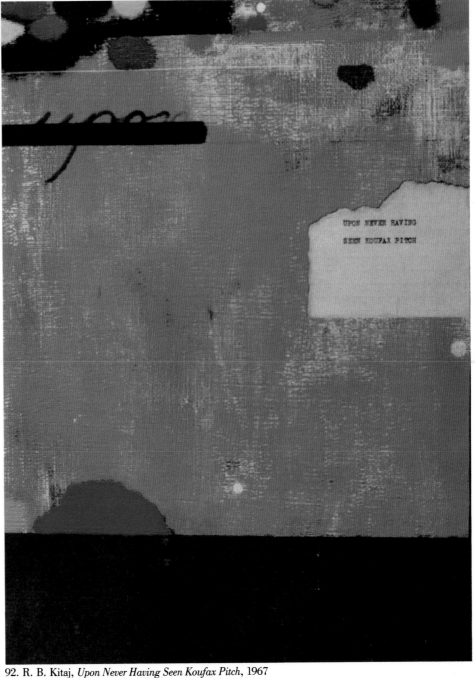

92. R. B. Kitaj, *Upon Never Having Seen Koufax Pitch*, 1967

more easily accessible than boxes of statistics. Merkin is an artist whose passion for expressed detail and for baseball is overt and entertaining.

Baseball is a sport whose outcome is in doubt until the very last pitch is thrown. When spring training is in progress, the soothsayers come out of their winter doldrums with well-documented analyses. They review the records and the schedules; they juggle the veterans and the newcomers and make their accustomed preseason predictions. More often than not, they are wrong. They can't foresee, for example, the extraordinary virtuosity of a player just coming into his prime, or the silly errors of the steady old-hands, or the serious injuries. Spring training is not all cool calculation, however. There is always the warm Southern sun and the undemanding goodwill of the vacationing spectators. Red Grooms's (b. 1937) watercolor "Spring Training in West Palm Beach" (1985) [Fig. 93] views the ball field through the protective mesh behind home plate, catching the action of a lively play. The bright and airy colors are reflective of Florida's pervasive light, while the cheerful atmosphere and exuberant fielding evoke baseball's original intent. The suitcase at the feet of the upcoming batter must surely signify a trip to another team.

Even a club's move to a new baseball-hungry city becomes a statistical factor. Sometimes it means a nose dive. The Dodgers sank to seventh place the year

93. Red Grooms, *Spring Training in West Palm Beach*, 1985

94. Kim MacConnel, *The Sliding Series*, 1980

95. Tony King, *Pitcher*, 1978

97. Nicholas Africano, *Ernie Banks*, 1979

96. Tony King, *Batter*, 1978

98. George Hartman, *The Orioles Win the Series*, 1966

they arrived in Los Angeles. Sometimes it signifies success. The lackluster St. Louis Browns had had a sorry professional history, years of total inertia, and a latter-day general manager, Bill Veeck, who brought in midgets and clowns, non-baseball paraphernalia and gadgets to puff up attendance. It simply did not work because baseball fanatics are just that: baseball fanatics. After years of futile attempts, the financially debilitated club was finally granted permission to sell its franchise to Baltimore in 1954. It became, with considerable pride, the Baltimore Orioles, a name of significance in baseball history, and proceeded to develop its own persona. In 1966, the underdog Baltimore Orioles not only won the American League pennant with grace and style, but they also took the World Series from the well-entrenched Los Angeles Dodgers in four games, holding them scoreless for an unheard-of thirty-three innings. It was a distinct shock, especially to the springtime prognosticators. The Dodgers had superior pitching, skilled and dangerous hitters, and prior World Series experience...and yet they lost.

If some artists took a broad philosophical view of the game and its relationship to societal problems and illusions, there were still those who remained true to the optimistic American scene, providing faithful pictorial records and information with verve and good humor. George Hartman (1894–1976) was undoubtedly excited by the 1966 rivalry. He must have returned to his studio and painted "The Orioles Win the Series" (1966) [Fig. 98] on the spot. He depicts number five, Brooks Robinson, the Orioles' great third baseman, literally jumping in the air with glee. He's upward bound; the only difficulty is that Hartman can't seem to get him down. His two equally ecstatic teammates are stampeding toward him, arms outstretched, ready for bear hugs of self-congratulation. The action is reproduced against the tightly painted, nonfigurative backdrop, representing a packed house.

MUNDANE MATTER AND ELEGANT IMAGERY

Post-1970s artists have defined their own perimeters and critics have offered new classifications: abstraction, construction, photo-realism, minimal art, neo-expressionism, pattern painting, naturalism. Whatever the descriptive term, art has adapted to the natural free flow of ideas inherent in an historic continuum. Acceptance of aesthetic experimentation and

interest in the lifestyles of the artists have mushroomed in direct proportion to the excitement generated by the surrounding hoopla and happenings. The media sends the message. Artists have joined athletes in superstar status and acclaim. With the open exchange of creative concepts, the educational input of the artists themselves, and the availability and diversity of their works, a visual dynamic of remarkable intensity has been added to public awareness. The contemporary art world is no longer an elitist sanctuary.

Still-life painter Lisa Dinhofer (b. 1952) has moved the basic implements of outdoor game playing indoors for her painting "Spring Street Hardball" (1988) [Fig. 100]. The configurations of objects, elegantly set on antique lace and silk, communicate the enjoyment of leisure activity and the intrinsic beauty of the ordinary tools of the games, so often disregarded. Dinhofer moves back and forth in time, creating different sequences and analogies. There are keepsakes and treasures, those welcome repositories of memories, and there are the bright, vivid reflections of the future: baseballs, scuffed and brand-new, commemorative baseballs of silver and crystal, multicolored marbles ablaze with the vibrancy of daylight and catching the glow of the brilliantly colored fabrics that support them, a milk-glass tennis ball, and a fortune-teller's crystal ball. They are all in harmony, symbolic evocations of the past and the future. Each of the two clear-glass balls carries an image of the city street into the studio, their reflections surprisingly upside down. The silver ball contains the artist's self-portrait, a firm, stabilizing element. While the work, in historic perspective, is emblematic of the traditionally lush viewpoint of nineteenth-century still-life painting, the hard edges and conceptual arrangements are distinctly concerned with today's movement toward perceptual realism.

Granted the wide-ranging styles, artists feel a freedom to explore areas other than those with which the major body of their work has been concerned. Ralph Goings (b. 1928) has long been considered a cool photo-realist, a detached observer, utilizing the emotionless clarity of a camera lens to capture in instant replay the very ordinary centers of everyday living. He depicts diner counters, gas pumps, pickup trucks, with their shiny chrome-plated surfaces, garish colors, and well-worn appearance, the necessary accoutrements of a mechanical age, and he translates them into the environment of art. His watercolor "Base-

99. Ralph Goings, *Baseball*, 1988

Going 88

100. Lisa Dinhofer, *Spring Street Hard Ball*, 1988

120

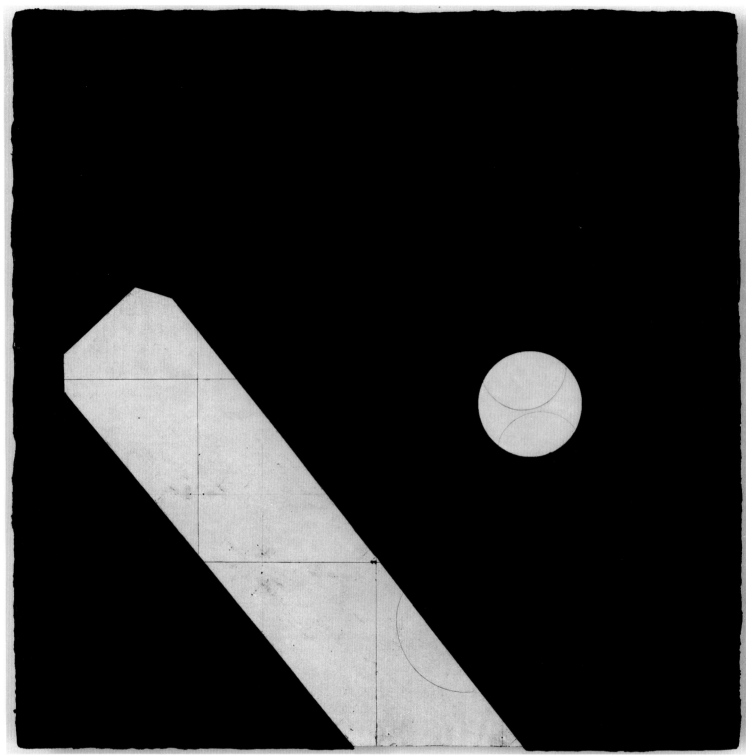

101. Donald Sultan, *Baseball and Bat*, 1981

102. Robert Kushner, *L.A. Dodgers*, 1978

ball" (1988) [Fig. 99] is a departure. Although a known instrument of lively play, the baseball is accorded a singular monumentality, highly unusual for this artist. The ball is firmly placed on a straight support between two unfocused windows, its bright-red laces dropping into the dense shadow beneath. It stands isolated, out of the context of the game, but nevertheless retaining its own quality of character and purposefulness.

Color plays an omnipresent role in the work of another gathering of artists who employ quick dabs of brilliant tones to bring closely related forms in and out of consciousness. Robert Kushner (b. 1946) portrayed the "L.A. Dodgers" (1978) [Fig. 102] as a crazy quilt of virtually undefinable decorative imagery, with the color patches of unrelieved intensity providing an active if diffused focus.

One step beyond projections of the commonplace standards of this mechanistic society is the relationship of industrial matter to the development of an image. Donald Sultan (b. 1951), emerging from early minimalist influences, experimented with functional modern materials totally irrelevant to the established painting processes. He glued linoleum tiles to wood, surfaced them with tar, and, when necessary, used industrial tools to formalize the imagery. His "Baseball and Bat" (1981) [Fig. 101] is set in an opaque ground. The bat is angular, flattened against the heavy backdrop, and tilted so that the lines where the tiles join appear as cross-hatchings on its face; a simple penciled arc signifies the place where ball and bat met. The ball has moved, a floating moon across this black eternity. There is a serenity in its flight which adds a subtle poetic dimension to the artistry of the national pastime.

1988: THE CONTEMPORARY CONTINUUM

Just when it appears that this automated, space-oriented society is no longer interested in the playthings of its youth, the underdog tradition takes hold, mesmerizing the entire nation. 1988's Los Angeles Dodgers were deemed a team of minor talent and lesser ambition. The combined wisdom of sportswriters and newscasters alike was that the team would never make the National League's division playoffs, but they did. The pundits then declared that, without a doubt, the New York Mets were a more professional, more sophisticated ensemble; the Mets lost after seven hard-fought games. Those same omniscient onlookers, reiterating their original theo-

103. Jeffrey Rubin, *Dave Winfield*, 1988

retical analyses, maintained that it was all happenstance, that the Dodgers were already played out, that they had exhausted their bull pen and their bench. The expectation was that the American League's powerhouse Oakland Athletics would grind them up in World Series play. Five games later, the Los Angeles Dodgers were the World Series Champions. The experts called it a managerial feat; but the record books will declare it a team effort. As tradition would have it, a new hero emerged. The young, clean-cut, controlled Dodger pitcher Orel Hershiser, for this series at least, demonstrated that he had it all: stamina, fast ball, slider, fielding abil-

ity, and hitting prowess. He achieved the Series's Most Valuable Player award and an honored place in baseball history. Today, there is an additional edge to the paeons of praise and national glory that such attainments warrant, and it leads directly to the considerable financial rewards of the off-season dinner-lecture circuit. Baseball remains an entertainment after all.

As for the hard-driving New York Mets and the coolly dedicated Oakland Athletics of 1988, who so swiftly toppled from top to underdog status, ultimately their pain will be assuaged and their losses vindicated. There's always the next decade or the next century, if not tomorrow.

104. John Dobbs, *Play at the Plate*, 1980

105. John Hull, *Minor League All Star Game: Clinton*, 198

106. *Baseball Watch*, c. 1900   *Baseball Watchstand*, c. 1910

Part Five

Artisans and entrepreneurs recognized the commercial as well as the aesthetic possibilities of baseball imagery from the very outset. The public's overwhelming passion for the game was self-evident and easily translated into sales, if the pitch was right. Versatile craftspeople and promoters weren't interested in interpreting or enlarging upon America's grand vision; they were simply encouraging American free enterprise.

CRAFTS: INDIVIDUAL IMPRESSIONS AND MASS-PRODUCED DECORATIVE ART

Baseball themes in folk and decorative art and in utilitarian domestic objects entered the cultural mainstream and the home through circuitous routes in the nineteenth century. Folk art of this genre remained a viable alternative to fine art imagery primarily because it portrayed, with understandable clarity, the pleasure of leisure experience and was relatively inexpensive to own as well. Reflecting the centuries-old craft tradition, many of these objects were conceived and sold by people with little òr no formal training in the arts. Their intent was to please a not very critical mass audience and thereby earn a decent wage. They didn't consider themselves fine artists; their trade title was designated by the craft they pursued. There were whittlers and carvers, sign painters and toy makers, potters and ironcasters, quilters and jewelry designers, among other artisans, with a vast array of talent. They all were attempting to ride baseball's crest and reach for the American miracle of financial success. Their modes of operation varied; some were itinerants and peddlers plying their trade from town to town, others established their own workshops in flourishing communities, while those with a stronger entrepreneurial bent surveyed the marketplace, trained apprentices, employed assistants, and proceeded to develop lucrative cottage industries that eventually evolved into factories of mass production.

European-trained ship carvers were the most skillful and sought-after craftsmen in the lusty ports of the Northeast. They were responsible for carving the fanciful ornamentation and prows of the great clipper ships. Their rosters of apprentices and assistants grew with the demands of maritime expansion. With the advent of the speed-oriented Industrial Revolution, however, and in recognition of the limitations of their craft, they diversified, creating and wholesaling representative symbols of trade for the retail shops of merchants and mechanics whose businesses lined the bustling main streets. These emblems soon became the most significant sources of revenue for those in the business of carving.

During the last quarter of the nineteenth century, the cobblestoned streets were alive with the visual excitement generated by gilded, polychromed, three-dimensional figures standing provocatively in front of each shop, beckoning to the passersby. Sometimes the carvings were clear-cut descriptions of the wares to be had inside, but more often they were unabashedly enticing reflections of the tastes of the shopkeepers or the ability of the craftsmen. Barbershop poles, cobblers' shoes, watchmakers' clocks, Indians of every denomination, American eagles, dancing girls, and baseball players provided information for those who could not read, advertised products and services for shoppers in a hurry, and piqued the interest of promenading browsers who were merely out for a stroll.

Carvers were interested in technique and production, not aesthetics or ideology. They experimented until they found an image that sold well and then they stockpiled. According to Samuel A. Robb (1851–1928), a major carver of shop symbols in New York City, a process was developed that was quick and practical. The carvers preferred logs of white pine, although other easily available woods were used as well. They considered a foot a day to be good carving time. Another day was allotted for each foot of finishing and painting, and a total of twelve days was deemed sufficient for the completion of a six-foot figure. The formula was simple. An outline was drawn on the log, usually from a paper pattern. The trunk was blocked out with an axe, apportioned into appropriate spaces for the head, the body to the waist, thence to the knee, the legs, and the feet. The wood was then roughly hewn with a chisel and mallet, carefully following the grain. The torso was always one piece, with the arms separately attached and bolted. As the figure evolved, the finishing touches were put on with finer carving tools. These were not unique figures. The images were derived from old prints, colored lithographs, and on very rare occasions from original models. Since these figures were designed for the outdoors, they were repainted regularly with different details added to suit the whim of the purchaser. Prices were set according to condition; used or heavily overpainted figures sold for twenty-five dollars, and newly carved models went for fifty, seventy-five, or as much as one hundred dollars, depending on the amount of detailing and individuality required.

With the introduction and expansion of the tobacco industry, shops catering to cigar smokers proliferated and competition was intense. Tobacconists, recognizing the merchandizing advantages of advertising, became the carvers' biggest customers. While Indians were by far the most commonly designated images, other popular sources, including baseball players, were added to the carvers' repertoire.

Thomas V. Brooks (1828–1895) was one of the foremost master carvers in New York City. Active from 1847 to 1879, "Daddy" Brooks, as he was affectionately known, had an active workshop filled to capacity by numerous apprentices and assistants; many of whom (including Samuel A. Robb) eventually opened craft shops of their own. With good business acumen, Brooks left for Chicago in 1879 in order to restore and invigorate the shop-sign trade which had been destroyed by the great fire. His quest was successful and he remained active until 1890. The emblematic "Baseball Player" (c. 1870–75) [Fig. 107], attributed to Brooks, was the result of a special order placed by Briggs's, a sporting goods shop, variously located in New York City and Bridgeport, Connecticut. The name of the shop, along with two crossed bats and a ball, appear in a crest across the player's chest. Obviously a pitcher, he appears attentive and relaxed, holding the baseball in preparation for the underhand pitch. His uniform is beautifully finished, with knickers falling in graceful folds to just below the knees, a tribute to the carver's dexterity. The red stockings and cap add an attractive ingratiating element to the whole.

Samuel A. Robb's "Baseball Player" (c. 1888–1903) [Fig. 108] is a more formidable fellow, with piercing eyes and a solid, well-proportioned body. His stance is firm, ready, his bat in position, his feet properly aligned. He is either awaiting the pitch or the customer's entry into the tobacconist's shop. The figure exudes confidence and strength. His full, well-carved black mustache, identical to that of Brooks's figure and representative of current fashion, accentuates the masculine bearing. Though silently extended, an invitation is directed to the potential customer with the expectation of acceptance. Another overt symbol, a baseball, considerably larger than life-size, is precisely painted on the base. Robb's baseball player sends an adroit commercial message, as it

107. Thomas V. Brooks (attributed to), *Baseball Player*, c. 1870–75

108. Samuel A. Robb, *The Baseball Player*, 1888–1903

109. Theo I. Josephs, *Box Office Sign*, c. 1890

was meant to do. It also maintains a strictly sculptural presence of its own.

With the enactment of regulatory ordinances forbidding sidewalk obstructions, the trade symbols were forced indoors, no longer serving a constructive function. Diminished in importance, they were discarded, tossed into waste bins, or used for firewood. Gradually, they were replaced by overhanging signboards, designed by carpenters and painters using decorative motifs and a wealth of recognizable subject

110. Hoffman, *Leister's Official Base Ball Score*, 1892–99

matter, including landscapes, portraits, symbols, or simply the name and address of the shop owner.

The growing need for calligraphy and fancy lettering introduced a new dimension to the sign painter's trade. The boards had to provide explicit information, yet be inviting to the eye. They required ingenuity, tact, and, for the sake of variety, a rejection of rote imagery. It was an arduous task. On the rare occasions when the painter was completely satisfied with his endeavor, he affixed his signature.

As inscribed, the baseball "Box Office Sign" (c. 1890) [Fig. 109] was conceived and printed by Theo I. Josephs, a resident of Solder's (sic) Home. Since the centered letter is a baseball and bat, the inference drawn is that the box office referred to was selling tickets to games played at the Soldier's Home or nearby. An urn and a vase with flowers are incorporated into two other letters symbolic, perhaps, of winning and losing or of life and death.

"Leister's Official Base Ball Score" (c. 1895) [Fig. 110], signed by a Philadelphia sign painter named Hoffman, came from the Leister House, an inn in Huntingdon, Pennsylvania. Listed on the scoreboard are all the National League teams active during the period 1892 to 1899. Conceivably, it hung over the bar, providing the patrons with scores posted at regular intervals. The nameplates are interchangeable, allowing the barman or maid to deliver the information with comparative ease. In addition, the lettering is so distinct as to be easily read across a dimly lit room. The difference in style and emphasis of the letters at the very bottom of the board advertising TOBACCO AND CIGARS provides the practical sales pitch.

The craft of carving for personal gratification was handed down from generation to generation. Amateur carvers adapted this European tradition to American subjects, inevitably including baseball. These small decorative household objects were not designed as articles of commerce; they were usually displayed on mantlepieces or corner cabinets for the enjoyment of family and friends. The naive folk sculpture of a "Baseball Player" (c. 1910) [Fig. 112] may have been a reflection of the carver's own experience or, as the broad grin suggests, it may have been created as a tribute to a particularly successful neighborhood baseball hero. Even though the carver was obviously unschooled in proper anatomy, he was able to infuse the dapper figure with a spirited verve and good humor.

Baseball was a game of chance as well as skill, played by the sandlot kid with all the joy of natural ability and all the drama of possibility. Baseball was a game played one on one in amusement arcades and country carnivals, where the test of physical prowess pitted the pitching ace against the mechanical dummy for the prize. The barker called the shots, the money was placed, the ball was tossed overhand and fast. Success yielded the prize, a baseball

111. Oscar de Mejo, *Tagged*, 1980

card, and the pride of achievement.

"The Baseball Catcher" (c. 1910–30) [Fig. 114] is a life-sized carved mechanical figure properly attired in cotton uniform and sneakers. He has a devil-may-care demeanor, his cap is tilted at a rakish angle, his eyes are widely set and focused, and his face is painted into a permanent, almost menacing, leer. He crouches, knees bent. His hands, one mitted and one bare, are cupped, awaiting the ball. The dare is implicit, the tension off-setting. Right

down the middle, the ball smacks into the glove and the hands jerk together, imprisoning it. Bells go off or lights go on and the prize is won. The game is simple enough and satisfying. But there is an artistry to this evocative figure, an aesthetic sensibility that places its origins in the hands of an artist. Its time frame is hard to establish. The uniform design, the debonair twirl of the painted mustache, the quality of the carving, and the apparent personal involvement in its singular design suggest

the teens or the Twenties, though there were manufactured mechanical baseball figures called "Attaboys" that appeared as late as the 1930s.

The American folk experience and its replication in craft often transcended the marketplace. Weathervanes, popular since the inception of the republic, also derived from a European heritage. The first recorded weathervane, however, was ancient Greek in origin at a time when the winds were worshipped as purveyors of

112. *Baseball Player*, c. 1910

113. *Baseball Batter Weathervane*, n.d.

good or evil. As wind determinants and decorative ornaments, they were useful for centuries. They were made of whittled wood, wrought iron, cut sheet metal, and hammered copper. In the Middle Ages the distinctive symbols satisfied the fears of the superstitious, protected seafarers, and projected the growth of the harvest. The images varied with the times. Agricultural and patriotic themes vied with cockerels and horn-blowing Gabriels, with chanticleers and Dianas of the Hunt. By the end of the nineteenth century, weathervanes were ornamental enough to serve as trade symbols in addition to their original function; pigs represented the butchers' trade, schooners identified the shipbuilders, and so on. The craftsmen let their imaginations take hold. Industry and transportation overtook mythology and the Bible. The village smithy gave way to manufacturers, and soon hardware stores were selling weathervanes depicting fire engines and locomotives. Delightful images of pleasure were reproduced, among them horse-drawn racing sulkies and baseball players.

136

"The Baseball Batter Weathervane" (n.d.) [Fig. 113] is cut out of sheet metal and may well have served as a trade symbol for a sporting goods shop, or possibly indicated wind conditions for a small ball field. The batter is in a formal batting stance, ready for the elements. By virtue of his construction, he is not simply an ornamental identification. He could just as easily have been whirled by a riotous wind into a semblance of a grand play as have introduced a shopkeeper's merchandise. The directional apparatus indicating north, south, east, and west, which should have encircled the rod below the player, has been lost with time.

TAPESTRY AND TEXTURE IN FOLK ART PAINTING

Baseball has provided a rich tapestry of color and movement for folk art painters. These so-called naive artists relay their information with a direct, childlike simplicity, unfettered by the nuances of academic traditions. They express little

concern for the inevitable distortions of perspective, spacial relationships, color, and form, regarding the canvas as an open field for the exploration of personal viewpoints and experience.

Ralph Fasanella (b. 1914) was a union organizer, involved in the movement's early struggles for recognition and parity in the workplace. He identifies baseball as the people's pastime, a proletarian sport. Fasanella's painting "Night Game (Practice Time)" (1979) [Fig. 115] not only portrays a panorama of pregame activity on the field and in the stands, but also presents separate small vignettes of spectators entering the park, purchasing their tickets, riding the escalators. These representational studies are easily understood within the context of the larger painting and are fun to decipher. Fasanella is precise about small details: the batting and pitching cages, and the clock set at eight-thirty. However, the roster of players indicated on the scoreboard contains highly unlikely names for team play. Generations separate Ruth, Gehrig, Aaron, Hubbell, Campanella,

114. *Baseball Catcher, Amusement Arcade Figure*, n.d.

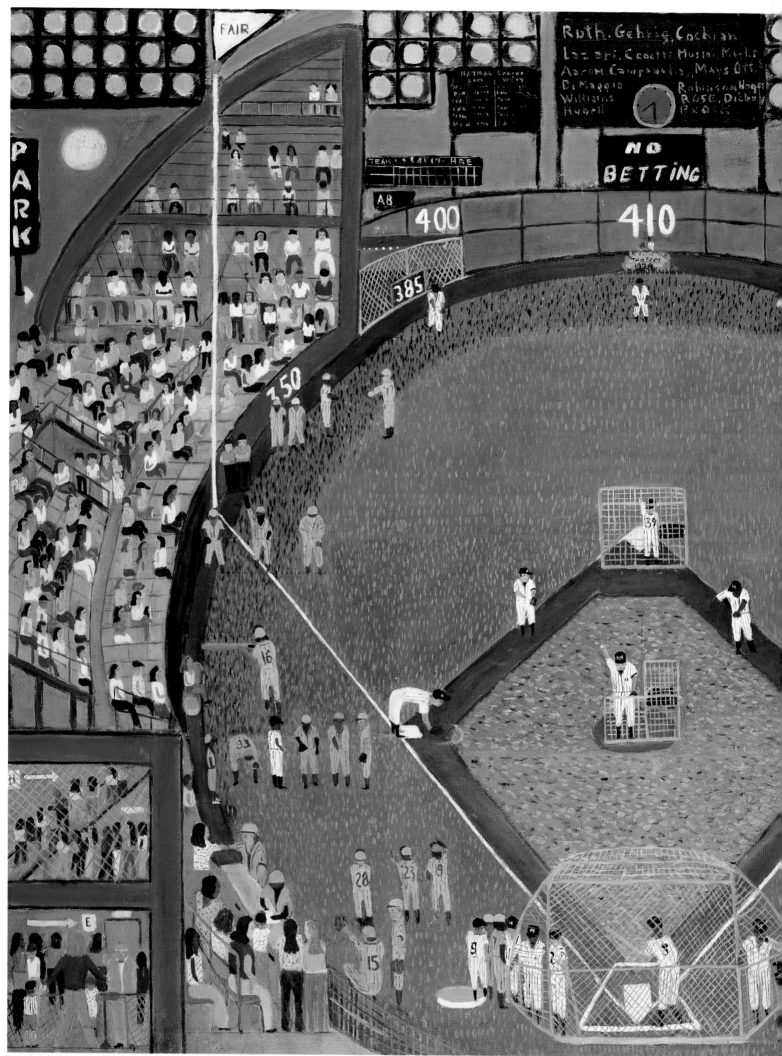

115. Ralph Fasanella, *Night Game (Practice Time)*, 1979

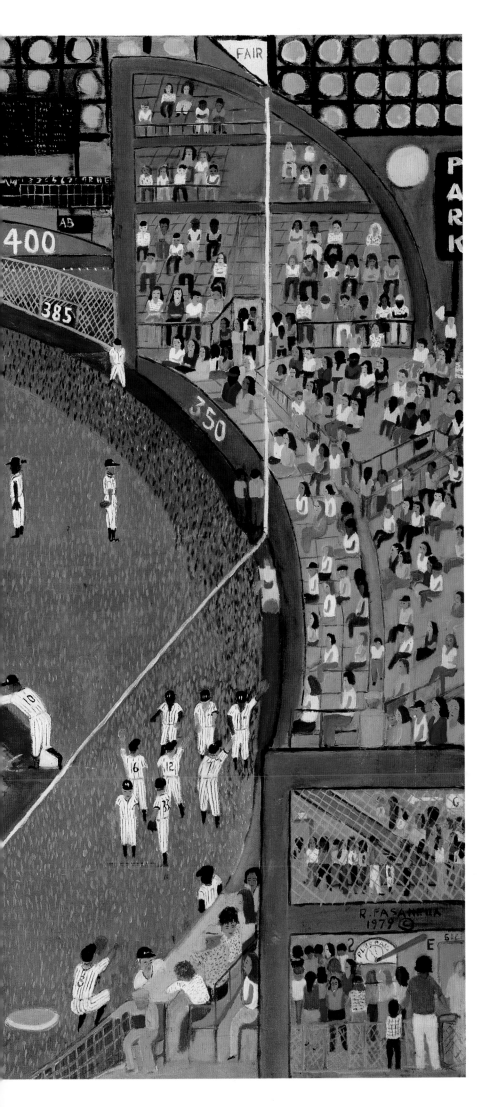

116. Gerald Garston, *Between Innings*, 1971

DiMaggio, Robinson, Ott, and the others. It is unreasonable but wonderful to imagine them all in a game together.

The general iconography of Oscar de Mejo's (b. 1911) folk painting is based less on observation than on a detached sense of the unreal. His figures are not balanced within the landscape; they protrude from trees, float through rooms on interior clouds, and play baseball with the graceful postures of ballet dancers. His painting "Tagged" (1980) [Fig. 111] is an anomaly. One player lies on a speed-generated cloud of dust, his face bearing the woebegone expression of failure, while another figure, ball in hand, is spread-eagled above him. The umpire, arms upraised, declares the out. The figures are totally out of proportion, but the play is realized with gusto.

BASEBALL AS EVERYDAY ENTERTAINMENT

Baseball lent itself easily to the formulation and design of toys and games for both adults and children. There were whirligigs and articulated figures, puppets and coin-operated games of chance. The original whirligigs were carved, animated devices brought to America as novelties. Single figures had loosely attached arms with hands shaped into paddles; more complex creations used several figures to project an event. The mechanical arrangements were similar to those of small windmills, mounted on boards and twirling rapidly when the wind's velocity reached a sufficient pitch. The "Baseball Game Whirligig" (n.d.) [Fig. 117] is hardly an accurate depiction of the game. Even the requisite number of players has not been fielded. It is the anticipation of an animated response to a natural force that generates the interest. The carver has managed to place his catcher in the customary crouch, the batter has his bat upraised, the pitcher stands with ball in hand, and as soon as the wind starts blowing, the game will commence.

If the whittler's single knife was handy and he was urged to enliven a dull evening's entertainment, he would quickly create an articulated figure, attach strings to the hands and feet, give it an absurd name, and allow his imagination to develop the story line. The "Articulated Baseball Figure" (n.d.) [Fig. 118] is crude and simple to an extreme. Still, the aquiline nose and steady stare, the bat lifted in preparation, the striped cap and socks endow the figure with an unexpected vigor and authenticity.

Imaginative armchair baseball players created their own games using mechanical

117. *Baseball Game Whirligig*, n.d.

devices and adult images. The metal "Mechanical Baseball Puppet" (n.d.) [Fig. 119] occupied a catcher's box on a large, simulated ball field set up in an armory. Puppets in the guise of team players, placed in proper positions on the diamond and mounted on wheels, were maneuvered by hand in order to reenact a game in progress while it was broadcast on the radio. There was a mechanism attached to the bodies that controlled arm movements. The hands contained slots for bulbs which lit up when there was a call. It was a variation of a chess board with less cerebral participation and more devotion to the game.

BASEBALL AT HOME

In the mid-nineteenth century, most American women were home centered, their lives limited by political omission and social expectation. Since the enhancement of family life and the provision of comfort and warmth were the valued roles, the old established crafts of quilting, embroidery, and textile design remained the women's province. The quilting bee, with its group involvement, was long considered a primarily social activity. Women created imaginative works of art with pieces of colored cotton, silk, and calico, and with dramatic sewing skills. Originally used solely as coverlets and counterpanes, quilts also provided visual excitement: developing narratives and histories, serving as albums and patriotic symbols, incorporating both flower forms and abstractions. Some quilters followed the traditional patterns and designs, while others brought their per-

118. *Articulated Baseball Figure*, n.d.

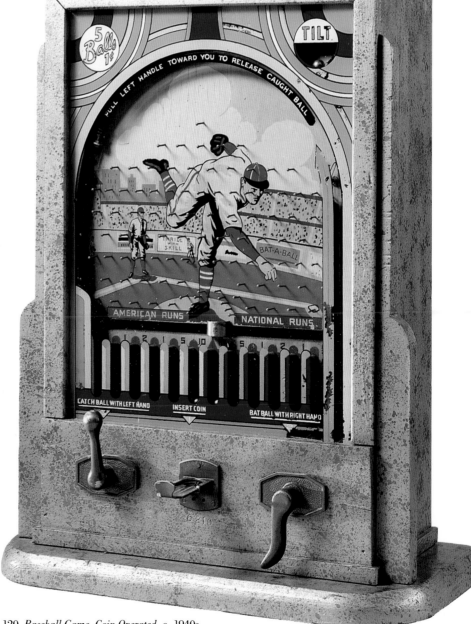

119. *Baseball Player, Mechanical Puppet*, c. 1910

120. *Baseball Game, Coin Operated*, c. 1940s

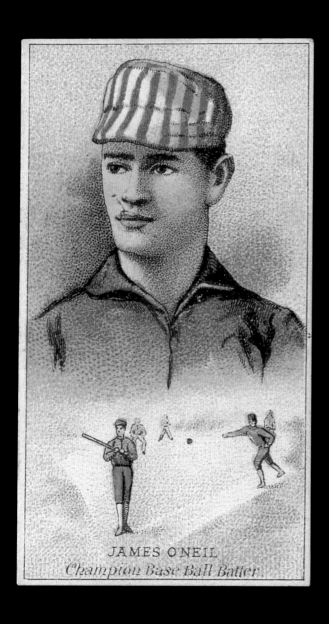

JAMES O'NEIL
Champion Base Ball Batter.

E. A. BURCH
Champion Base Ball Fielder.

121. *Baseball Cards* (four), W. S. Kimball & Co., 1887–88

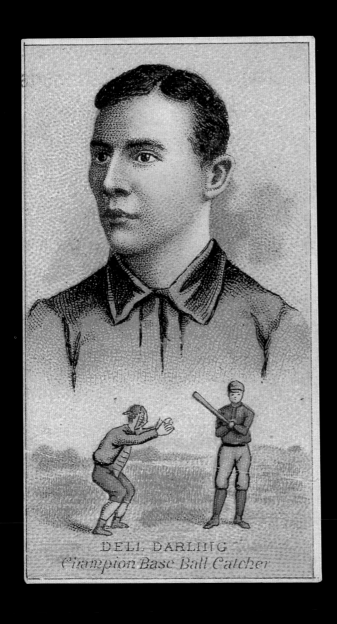

DELL DARLING
Champion Base Ball Catcher

HARDIE HENDERSON
Champion Base Ball Pitcher

sonal insights and creative energy into the group dynamic. Techniques varied with function; expert needlecraft was necessary for quilting design, while heavily embroidered blocks of patchwork and appliqued fanciful figures on the quilted surface not only supplied the necessary warmth but also enlivened an often-drab home.

The narrow "Baseball Quilt" (n.d.) [Fig. 126] was undoubtedly made for a young boy's bed. Beautifully quilted, the centered appliques of bats, mitt, and cap and the border of baseballs create a playful image within a formal layout. The patchwork "History of Baseball Quilt" (c. 1940) [Fig. 127] relates twelve episodes in the development of the game, from the initial patch, an illustration taken from the early-nineteenth-century *Book of Sports*, to the 1940s. The scenes are so clearly delineated and the fabric so neatly placed, however, that the pieces may well have come from a kit ready to be assembled and sewn. Nevertheless, a baseball document, brightly illuminated and lying across the bed, surely must have excited the interest of the entire household.

Printed textiles with baseball themes were not unique even at the beginning of this century. Cotton patches replicating portraits of prominent baseball figures were given as souvenirs with boxes of cigars. Their design was akin to the baseball cards that had already become the rage. When several of these patches were collected, they were pieced and worked into patchwork pillows or, as in the "Baseball Textile" (1910), [Fig. 124] decorative wall hangings.

Baseball entered the home and transformed that constricted environment through the sheer exuberance of its imagery. The mission oak "Baseball Bench" (probably early twentieth century) has an active full-scale baseball scene carved as a decorative frieze on its frame. To prove that baseball furniture was not just another idiosyncratic element of turn-of-the-century design, Silas Kopf (b. 1949), a contemporary craftsman and designer, fabricated a trompe l'oeil "Baseball Marquetry Cabinet" (1988) [Fig. 123] of east Indian laurel and walnut. Its door panels contain a still-life composition with basic baseball accoutrements, including bat, ball, mitt, cap, jersey, and trophy, in prominent, if deliberately haphazard, display. And for those homebound enthusiasts who preferred that their objects provide a real service, there was a scuffed white "Genuine Horsehide, Official League Ball" with "Cushion Cork Center," an actual "Baseball Radio" (c. 1930s) [Fig. 122] broadcasting

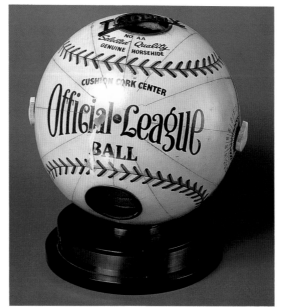

122. *Baseball Radio*, c. 1930s

123. Silas Kopf, *Baseball Marquetry Cabinet*, 1988

C'TOOLE PITT

COBB DETF

124. *Baseball Textile, Wallhanging,* c. 1910

125. *Brooklyn Dodger Sym-phony Drum*, c. 1948

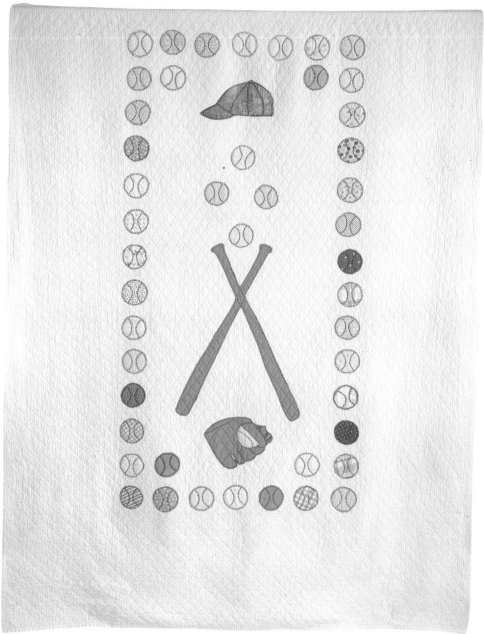

126. *Baseball Quilt*, n.d.

128. *Baseball Mission Bench*, n.d. (detail)

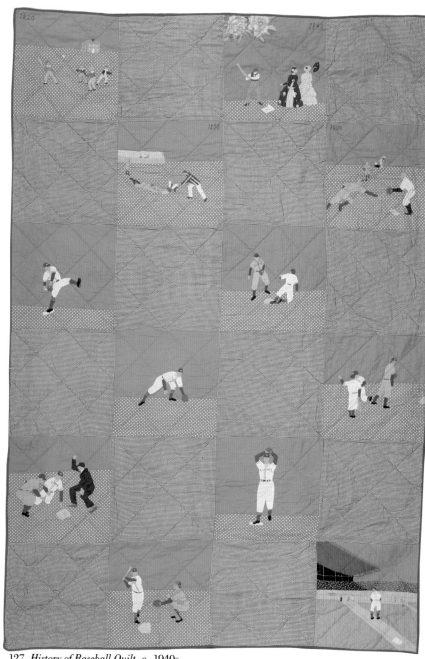

127. *History of Baseball Quilt*, c. 1940s

128. *Baseball Mission Bench*, n.d.

129. *Japanese Banner*, 1941–42

the games for eager listeners.

Items for personal adornment used baseball imagery as well. Women who wore their hair piled fashionably high in "Gibson Girl" style backed up their coiffures with decorative combs. The horn "Baseball Comb" (c. 1870) [Fig. 130] has delicate carving with images of two uniformed baseball players standing and two sliding into base, among other figures, all interlaced in the traditional intricately patterned Spanish style of design. And the men who carried hunter-case pocket watches as an indispensable part of their costume were provided with a helpful timepiece for a game in overtime. The "Baseball Watch" (1900) [Fig. 106], of French-niello on silver, depicts an elegant threesome in silhouette—the batter, catcher, and umpire—waiting for the play at the plate, with an engraved background of the crowded stands. Designed for display on a gentleman's bureau, the silver "Baseball Watchstand" (1910) [Fig. 106] makes a formal presentation. A figure dressed in nine-

teenth-century uniform stands to one side of the arch, hand lightly placed on hip, while directly in front of him a disheveled youngster carries a huge bat under one arm, just waiting to get on to the field.

From the boudoir to the living room, the artifacts of the game play a part in the most intimate aspects of everyday life. They are cheerful reminders that the advent of the spring season, with its heavy schedule of baseball games, is happily inevitable.

JAPAN AND THE INTERNATIONAL BASEBALL GAME

Baseball has developed a spectacular international following: Canada, Mexico, South America, and, particularly, Japan, where vast crowds attend games in Tokyo and other major cities. Although the Japanese players have been well trained and play the game with an impeccable professionalism, the glamour still remains with the American stars. They are eagerly sought after, coerced by bloated salaries to

demonstrate their native talents and to bask in the adulation of the Japanese fans. A belief, commonly held, is that the American occupation forces brought the game to Japan with them. However, there is documentary evidence that even in the rigid, restricted social and religious environment of pre-World War II Japan, the game of baseball was a prime attraction.

A fringed purple silk banner with a white appliqued baseball, gold crossed bats, and calligraphic details has recently come to view [Fig. 129]. According to the legends on the attached streamers, it was awarded semiannually to the winners of company baseball championships in Chong Kuo, Tsingtao Province, a central-eastern coastal town, located approximately 350 miles southeast of Beijing in Japanese-occupied China. The tournaments were sponsored by the local Tanaka Hardware Store. The Tsingtao Rubber Company team was honored in Fall 1941 and the Fuji Boseki (textile) Company team in Spring 1942.

130. *Baseball Comb*, c. 1870

EPILOGUE

Illusion, myth, and reality coexist in baseball's grand theatrical style. There is the dominating image of valor, the stalwart, steady-eyed hero who stands alone on the pitcher's mound, his calm demeanor belied by the tobacco juice dribbling down from the corners of his mouth. He touches his cap, fingers his jersey, fondles the ball, exchanging signals with the catcher. His adversary, equally worthy, is poised in the batter's box. Taut, edgy, glancing down the baseline, he waits for the coach's signal, swinging his bat into position. The duellers, for such they are, are contemplative and withdrawn, calculating each other's ability, intelligence, and cunning. The windup commences, the pitch is thrown. Watching intently, the umpire, the supreme arbiter, turns abruptly and makes the call: right down the middle, high, into the dirt, or outside. It's a strike or a ball; a line drive, a pop fly, or a home run. The field is suddenly a kaleidoscope of choreographed movement; players run, leap, stretch into the distance. The stands erupt in indiscriminate cheers and catcalls, then quiet: another inning, another confrontation, another game, another season. There is no lasting disappointment. Heroes will appear again; records will be broken; new championship teams will emerge; excitement will overwhelm...next year.

131. Fletcher Martin, *Out at Home*, 1940

LIST OF ILLUSTRATIONS

The name of every illustrated work is listed below, by the figure number as it appears in this book.

44. Philip Evergood
    "Early Youth of Babe Ruth," c. 1939
    oil on canvas, 20x24
    Hirshhorn Museum and Sculpture Garden,
        Smithsonian Institution
    Gift of Joseph H. Hirshhorn, 1966

45. Ben Shahn
    "Vacant Lot," 1939
    watercolor and gouache on paper mounted
        on panel, 19x23
    Wadsworth Atheneum, Hartford
    The Ella Gallup Sumner and Mary Catlin
        Sumner Collection

46. Jacob Lawrence
    "Strike," 1949
    tempera on masonite, 20x24
    Permanent Collection, Gallery of Art,
        Howard University, Washington D.C.

47. Robert Riggs
    "The Impossible Play," 1949
    oil on wood panel, 10¾x31⅝
    Estelle C. and Arnold J. Kaplan

48. Philip Evergood
    "Come and Help Grandad," 1944
    oil on canvas, 28¾x39½
    Sid Deutsch Gallery

49. Edward Laning
    "Saturday Afternoon at Sportsman's Park," 1944
    oil on canvas, 36x32
    The Gladstone Collection of Baseball Art

50. Nelson Rosenberg
    "Out at Third," n.d.
    watercolor and gouache on paper, 15x21⅞
    The Phillips Collection, Washington D.C.

51. Louis Bouché
    "Baseball Game, Long Island," 1939
    oil on canvas, 20x25
    The Metropolitan Museum of Art,
    George A. Hearn Fund, 1940

52. Ferdinand E. Warren
    "Night Ball Game," 1946
    oil on canvas, 32x47
    Georgia Museum of Art, The University of
        Georgia
    Eva Underhill Holbrook Memorial Collection of
        American Art
    Gift of Alfred H. Holbrook, GMOA 47.174

53. Henry Koerner
    "Rose Arbor," 1947
    oil on composition board, 27¾x35
    The Museum of Modern Art, New York
    Gift of John Hay Whitney

54. Seymour Leichman
    "Fate Takes a Hand," 1969
    color lithograph, 30x22½
    Photograph courtesy of
        Kennedy Galleries, Inc., New York

55. William Crawford
    "Termites in the Temple," c. 1946
    pen and ink on paper, 22½x19
    The Gladstone Collection of Baseball Art

56. James Chapin
    "Man on First," 1948
    oil on canvas, 28x24
    The Gladstone Collection of Baseball Art

57. Norman Rockwell
    "The Dugout," 1948
    watercolor, 19x17⅞
    The Brooklyn Museum
    Gift of Kenneth Stuart

58. Roy Lichtenstein
    "Baseball Manager," 1963
    oil and magna on canvas, 68x58
    Blum Helman Gallery, New York

59. Joseph Delaney
    "Brooklyn Bums Clubhouse," 1955
    charcoal on cardboard, 24x30
    Ewing Gallery of Art and Architecture,
        University of Tennessee, Knoxville

60. Leo O'Mealia
    "Who's a Bum!," 1955
    ink on board, 15x10
    The Gladstone Collection of Baseball Art

61. David Levine
    "Leo Durocher," 1973
    ink on paper, 13½x11
    Forum Gallery, New York
    Reprinted with permission from
        The New York Review of Books
    ©1973 NYrev, Inc.

62. Willard Mullin
    "Brooklyn Bum," n.d.
    watercolor, 15x17½
    The Gladstone Collection of Baseball Art

63. Robert Weaver
    "Ebbets Field," 1981 (2)
    pen and acrylic on paper, 7½x7
    Collection of the Artist

64. Seymour Chwast
    "The Grand Game of Baseball...and the
        Brooklyn Dodgers," 1987
    offset lithograph, 24x36
    Private Collection

65. Norman Rockwell
    "Study for 'Bottom of the Sixth'," c. 1940s
    oil on canvas, 16¼x15½
    Daniel M. Galbreath

66. Elaine de Kooning
    "Campy at the Plate," 1953–1980
    acrylic on canvas, 30x39½
    Collection of the Artist

67. Frederick Weinberg
    "Baseball Player" c. 1950
    painted metal, 27x17½
    The Gladstone Collection of Baseball Art

68. Andy Jurinko
    "Ebbets Field," 1983
    charcoal and pastel on paper, 30x44
    Kidder Peabody & Co.

69. David Levine
    "Crowd at Ebbets Field," c. 1960
    oil on canvas, 29x36
    Forum Gallery, New York
    ©1989 by David Levine

70. Lance Richbourg
    "Jackie Robinson," 1988
    oil on canvas, 72x87
    O. K. Harris Gallery

71. Andy Jurinko
    "Dodger Lumber of '54," 1985
    oil on canvas, 62x80
    Robert Sui

72. Kendall Shaw
    "Four at Bat," 1964
    acrylic on canvas, 68x96
    Collection of the Artist

73. Al Hirschfeld
    "Casey Stengel Teaches Samuel Johnson
        How to Speak," c. 1965
    pen and ink and wash, 28x26
    The Margot Feiden Galleries
    Mr. and Mrs. Philip S. Straniere

74. Justin McCarthy
    "World Series 1952 New York Yankees vs.
        Brooklyn Dodgers," 1952
    watercolor on board, 21½x28
    The Gladstone Collection of Baseball Art

75. Rhoda Sherbell
    "Charles Dillon (Casey) Stengel," 1981
    polychromed bronze, 44 H
    The National Portrait Gallery, Smithsonian
        Institution

76. Norman Rockwell
    "The Rookie," 1957
    oil on canvas, 41x39
    Judy Goffman Fine Art, New York City

77. John Kennard
    "Batting Coach, Little Falls, N.Y.," 1983
    photograph, 18x12
    Collection of the Artist

78. Raoul Dufy
    "Ball Park—Boston," c. 1950
    watercolor, 19½x25½
    Rose Art Museum, Brandeis University,
        Waltham, Massachusetts
    Gift of Mr. and Mrs. Edwin E. Hokin

79. Robert Gwathmey
    "County Stadium (World Series)," 1958
    oil on canvas, 32½x45½
    Terry Dintenfass Gallery

80. Marjorie Phillips
    "Night Baseball," 1951
    oil on canvas, 24¼x36
    The Phillips Collection, Washington D.C.

81. Tim Woodman
    "Practice," 1988
    painted aluminum, 33½x20x8½
    The Gladstone Collection of Baseball Art

82. John Fawsett
    "My Favorite Artist—Steinberg," 1986
    collage, 22x28½
    The Gladstone Collection of Baseball Art

83. Saul Steinberg
    "Corrugated Catcher," 1954
    mixedmedia, 30x30
    Jason van Dalen

84. Robert Rauschenburg
    "Canto XXIX: Illustration for Dante's 'Inferno',"
        1959–60
    pastel, gouache, watercolor and pencil,
        14⅝x11½
    The Museum of Modern Art, New York
    Given anonymously

85. Claes Oldenburg
    "Bat Spinning at the Speed of Light," 1975
    lithograph, 35½x22¼
    The Gladstone Collection of Baseball Art

86. Claes Oldenburg
   "Maquette for Batcolumn," 1975
   welded and painted steel on steel base,
   39½x12x12
   National Museum of American Art,
      Smithsonian Institution
   Transfer from General Services Administration

87. Ernest Trova
   "Baseball," c. 1960
   oil on canvas, 16x14
   The Gladstone Collection of Baseball Art

88. Andy Warhol
   "Baseball," 1962
   Silkscreen ink and oil, 91½x82
   Nelson-Adkins Museum of Art

89. Leigh A. Wiener
   "The Giant Killer," 1963
   silver print, 11x14
   The Witkin Gallery, Inc., New York City

90. Wayne Thiebaud
   "Hats," 1988
   oil on paper, 19x18
   Allan Stone Gallery

91. Richard Merkin
   "Kirby Higbe (22-9), Whit Wyatt (22-10) and the
      Pitching Staff of the National League Champion
      Brooklyn Dodgers, 1941, Minus Tamulis," 1967
   mixed media, 60x80
   Carol R. and Avram J. Goldberg

92. R. B. Kitaj
   "Upon Never Having Seen Koufax Pitch," 1967
   oil on canvas, 14⅛x10
   Private Collection

93. Red Grooms
   "Spring Training in West Palm Beach," 1985
   watercolor, 14x17
   Andrea and Barry D. Wendroff

94. Kim MacConnel
   "The Sliding Series," 1980
   two-color silk screen on die cut and folded paper,
      23x28½
   Holly Solomon Gallery

95. Tony King
   "Pitcher," 1978
   photographic emulsion and gouache, 10x10
   Collection of the Artist

96. Tony King
   "Batter," 1978
   photographic emulsion and gouache, 10x10
   Collection of the Artist

97. Nicholas Africano
   "Ernie Banks," 1979
   acrylic on canvas, 13x32½
   Holly Solomon Gallery

98. George Hartman
   "The Orioles Win the Series," 1966
   oil on canvas, 14x18
   D. Wigmore Fine Arts, New York

99. Ralph Goings
   "Baseball," 1988
   watercolor on foam core, 5¼x5¼
   The Gladstone Collection of Baseball Art

100. Lisa Dinhofer
   "Spring Street Hard Ball," 1988
   oil on canvas, 25x40
   The Gladstone Collection of Baseball Art

101. Donald Sultan
   "Baseball and Bat," 1981
   oil and graphite on tile over wood, 48⅝x48½
   Blum Helman Gallery, New York

102. Robert Kushner
   "L.A. Dodgers," 1978
   acrylic on paper, 66¾x30⅛
   Holly Solomon Gallery

103. Jeffrey Rubin
   "Dave Winfield," 1988
   oil on black-and-white photograph, 41x56
   O. K. Harris Gallery

104. John Dobbs
   "Play at the Plate," 1980
   oil on canvas, 26x30
   Collection of the Artist

105. John Hull
   "Minor League All Star Game: Clinton," 1988
   acrylic on canvas, 24x36
   Grace Borgenicht Gallery, New York

106. Baseball Watch, c. 1900
   French Niello on silver, 1⅞x1⅞
   The Gladstone Collection of Baseball Art

106. Baseball Watchstand, c. 1910
   silver, 5½x4x1½
   The Gladstone Collection of Baseball Art

107. Thomas V. Brooks (attributed to)
   "Baseball Player (Shop Sign)," c. 1870–75
   polychromed wood, 70½ H
   Hood Museum of Art, Dartmouth College,
      Hanover, N.H.
   Gift of Abby Aldrich Rockefeller

108. Samuel A. Robb
   "The Baseball Player," 1888–1903
   polychromed wood, 78x16½x14
   Heritage Plantation of Sandwich

109. Theo I. Josephs
   "Box Office Sign," c. 1890
   polychromed wood, 11⅜x48¼
   The Gladstone Collection of Baseball Art

110. (no first name) Hoffman
   "Leister's Official Base Ball Score"
      1892-99
   polychromed wood, 80x40
   The Gladstone Collection of Baseball Art

111. Oscar de Mejo
   "Tagged," 1980
   acrylic on masonite, 16x20
   Aberbach Fine Art

112. Baseball Player, c. 1910
   wood, 15x6x3½
   The Gladstone Collection of Baseball Art

113. Baseball Batter Weathervane, n.d.
   metal, 17x39
   The Gladstone Collection of Baseball Art

114. Baseball Catcher, Amusement Arcade
      Figure, n.d.
   wood, metal, cloth, leather, 52x26x30
   The Gladstone Collection of Baseball Art

115. Ralph Fasanella
   "Night Game (Practice Time)," 1979
   oil on canvas, 40x50
   Collection of the Artist

116. Gerald Garston
   "Between Innings," 1971
   silkscreen, 20x20
   Philadelphia Museum of Art
   Gift of Pucker-Safrai Gallery, Boston

117. Baseball Game Whirligig, n.d.
   polychromed wood, 18x36x10
   The Gladstone Collection of Baseball Art

118. Articulated Baseball Figure, n.d.
   polychromed wood, 24x9x4½
   The Gladstone Collection of Baseball Art

119. Baseball Player Mechanical Puppet, c. 1910
   metal and cloth, 34x6x3½
   The Gladstone Collection of Baseball Art

120. Baseball Game, Coin Operated, c. 1940s
   polychromed metal, 25x17x7¾
   The Gladstone Collection of Baseball Art

121. Baseball Cards (four), W. S. Kimball & Co.,
      1887–88
   cardboard, 1½x2¾ (each)
   The Gladstone Collection of Baseball Art

122. Baseball Radio, c. 1930s
   paper, metal, and leather, 9½x9½
   The Gladstone Collection of Baseball Art

123. Silas Kopf
   "Baseball Marquetry Cabinet," 1988
   east Indian laurel and walnut, 85x29¾x18½
   The Gladstone Collection of Baseball Art

124. Baseball Textile, Wallhanging, c. 1910
   printed cotton, 22x22½
   Cooper-Hewitt Museum, The Smithsonian
      Institution's National Museum of Design
   Gift of Mr. and Mrs. Stephen Smith

125. Brooklyn Dodger Sym-phony Drum, c. 1948
   polychromed wood, metal, and canvas,
      13x14x26
   The Gladstone Collection of Baseball Art

126. Baseball Quilt, n.d.
   homespun and cotton, 86x68
   The Gladstone Collection of Baseball Art

127. History of Baseball Quilt, c. 1940s
   cotton, 96x62
   The Gladstone Collection of Baseball Art

128. Baseball Mission Bench, n.d.
   wood, 38½x45x22½
   The Gladstone Collection of Baseball Art

129. Japanese Banner, 1941–42
   silk, 42x30
   The Gladstone Collection of Baseball Art

130. Baseball Comb, c. 1870
   horn, 7½x7½
   The Gladstone Collection of Baseball Art

131. Fletcher Martin
   "Out at Home," 1940
   oil on canvis, 23¼x44
   © 1979 Sotheby's, Inc.

ARTISTS' INDEX

The name of each artist is listed below. Page numbers indicate where each name appears in the book. Numbers in italics refer to illustrations.